ESSENTIAL
INSTANT™ VORTEX™
AIR FRYER OVEN
COOKBOOK

ESSENTIAL
INSTANT™ VORTEX™
AIR FRYER OVEN
COOKBOOK

100 RECIPES FOR AIR FRYING, ROASTING, DEHYDRATING, ROTISSERIE & MORE

OFFICIAL
Instant
BOOK

DONNA-MARIE PYE

Robert
ROSE

For complete cataloging information, see page 183.

DESIGN AND PRODUCTION: Kevin Cockburn/PageWave Graphics Inc.
EDITOR: Kathleen Fraser
INDEXER: Gillian Watts

The publisher gratefully acknowledges the financial support of our publishing program by the Government of Canada through the Canada Book Fund.

Canada

Published by Robert Rose Inc.
120 Eglinton Avenue East, Suite 800, Toronto, Ontario, Canada M4P 1E2
Tel: (416) 322-6552 Fax: (416) 322-6936
www.robertrose.ca

Printed and bound in Canada

1 2 3 4 5 6 7 8 9 MI 28 27 26 25 24 23 22 21 20

MIX
Paper from
responsible sources
FSC® C103567
FSC www.fsc.org

CONTENTS

PREFACE

It's been 20 years since I published my first cookbook, *Canada's / America's Best Slow Cooker Recipes*, and I still continue to be a fan of this indispensable cooking appliance. So when my publisher approached me with an opportunity to write a new appliance cookbook, I was somewhat hesitant. But as I learned more about this new kitchen magician about to hit the market, I decided to take the leap into the world of Vortex.

My first introduction arrived one snowy day in January, when my friend Linnea Scian made a quick drive to Buffalo, New York, to pick up a few ovens, since they could not yet be procured in Canada. No sooner was it out of the box, my son Jack had some cheese sticks breaded and freezing and ready to air fry. The next night, he and I prepared some chicken wings and brushed them with a prepared barbecue sauce I had in my refrigerator. After that feed, we decided they were a definite must-have recipe for the cookbook (see Bacon-Wrapped Chicken Wings with Beer Smear Sauce, page 34). And on it went. I made rotisserie chicken, just like the grocery store deli takeout variety, french fries — crispy on the outside, and hot and tender on the inside — and perfectly puffed cinnamon sugar–coated churros. The

more I experimented, the more delightful taste sensations became a reality.

Of course, the benefit of the Vortex Plus (7-in-1), and the Vortex Pro (9-in-1), is that this is so much more than an air fryer. It roasts, bakes, broils and toasts (Pro), plus proofs (Pro), dehydrates, rotates and reheats. It's the perfect appliance if you live in a small condo and have minimal cooking space, or if you are on your own or in a smaller household, and if you don't want to spend the time or energy to heat a large oven. It's healthy, clean, efficient and fast — a lot faster than a slow cooker.

I have included many favorite recipes that we traditionally think of as "fried," such as the Best Buttermilk-Brined Fried Chicken (page 100) and Buffalo Cauliflower Bites with Blue Cheese Dip (page 38). Using the rotate function and the convenient rotisserie spit created succulent roasted meats such as Thai Rotisserie Chicken (page 98) and Jamaican Jerk Rotisserie Pork (page 73), while the rotisserie basket attachment produced perfectly crisp Marinated Brussels Sprouts with Bacon (page 145) and golden brown fries in my The Best Fries (page 150) recipe. Throughout these pages you will find out-of-the-ordinary recipes such as Avocado Fries with Lime Sriracha

Dip (page 32) and Crispy Deviled Eggs (page 35), and healthy vegetarian and vegan options such as Spinach Salad with Crispy Tofu (page 136) and Mexicali Quinoa Stuffed Peppers (page 128), that take next to no time to prepare in the Vortex. (Look for the icons that identify vegan **V**, gluten-free **GF** and dairy-free **DF** recipes.)

Of course, all this would not have been possible without an amazing team of friends and colleagues who were willing to jump in and help! Thanks to my technical wizard, organizer and Girl Friday friend, Linnea Scian, who happily drove to Buffalo to pick up machines and spent hours tabulating recipes and creating a working spreadsheet so that testing could be done efficiently and on target. And to my recipe-testing team of Jean Stacey, Allison McCarthy, Janet Ruetz and Lynne Barna, who always wore smiles, even when I said, "Okay, let's try that recipe again, only this time...." Thank you to my Relish Cooking Studio team, especially my business partner, Maria Burjoski, who took over the reins for me for three months and allowed me the time to develop, test and write recipes while she tended the fires and singlehandedly managed things when I wasn't always available.

And of course, as always, thank you to my loving and supportive family — son Jack, who happily taste tested everything, and husband Lawrence, who nudged me to early-morning writing sessions when it felt as if I had just climbed into bed late the night before after having taught a cooking class. And thanks to my daughter, Darcy, who cheered me on from afar, constantly checking in to see how the book was progressing and how I was feeling at the same time.

Thank you to my Robert Rose family — publisher Bob Dees, who couldn't believe I agreed to do this project at a time when crazy things were happening in this world, and marketing coordinator Rachel Harry, who was always hungry and enthusiastic for the end result when I talked about the recipes I was working on. To Kevin Cockburn at PageWave Graphics for pulling this all together in such short timelines, and Kathleen Fraser, for her fantastic editorial work, making the words on paper seem like I know what I'm doing.

Writing a cookbook is like creating a great musical: it's a collaboration between actors and musicians and that's actually the pleasure of it — creating something together that you all love doing. Thank you, everyone. It's been a blast.

INTRODUCTION

Ready for the next home cooking revolution? Welcome to the world of the Instant Vortex, a 7-in-1 Plus, or 9-in-1 Pro, wonder fryer appliance that is an air fryer, rotisserie and dehydrator, but also bakes, roasts, broils and reheats with one simple touch. It's designed to make all your cooking fun, quick and effortless. Are you looking for new recipes? Perhaps you have heard about this new appliance and you're wondering if all the fuss is justified. Or maybe you've already unboxed your new Vortex, and it looks sleek and smart, but you don't know where to start. No matter your level of expertise, this cookbook is here to help. The instructions and recipes in this book will work with whatever model of Vortex you have.

Millions of people are already choosing air frying to make crisp, crunchy delicious fare, using just a spritz of oil and avoiding the health concerns associated with high-fat deep frying. The air fryer feature of the Vortex Plus and Vortex Pro uses hot air rather than hot oil to produce the same crispy, crunchy texture that makes deep frying so delectable. The blast of hot air traps all that juicy moisture beneath the crisp coating.

However, the Vortex is so much more than that. It is actually a countertop convection oven that can make almost any of your favorite dishes in about half the time it usually takes. You can create succulent self-basting roasts using the spit and equally crisp bites and nibbles with a hint of crunch using the rotisserie basket. You can cook a steak in less time than it takes to heat up a grill. You can reheat frozen foods or your favorite leftovers in less time with better results than your oven or microwave. And baking many classic treats like cakes and brownies just got so much simpler, using less time and energy than when made in a larger oven. The one-touch display panel allows you to customize and control the cooking time and temperature so your favorite meals can be made the way you like them.

What I cover in this book are some basic how-tos for maximum success, plus a generous selection of great recipes to get you started and take your meal prep to the next level. You'll find a description of all the Vortex Pro/Plus cooking functions and plenty of ideas on what you can use them for. I hope you will have as much fun preparing these recipes as I had creating them — and tasting them. Join the Vortex revolution and have fun in your kitchen!

SMART PROGRAMS

The Vortex Pro/Plus uses rapid air circulation to cook food, giving your meals the rich, crispy flavor you get from deep frying but with little or no oil. Let's review some important tips and the specific programs and what they are best suited for.

TIPS

- Each Smart Program has a default setting, so it's important to set your time and temperature before you press START. It's also important to note that Smart Programs automatically save your latest temperature and time setting.

- The Vortex Pro/Plus should always be preheated before adding food items, except when using the rotisserie setting. The cooking cycle will start once the ADD FOOD indicator displays, whether the food has been added or not. (The recipe times in this book include the preheating time.)

- Partway through the cooking process, the display will beep and show a TURN FOOD message. This is a reminder for you to take action: you will need to flip your food over on the cooking tray and adjust cooking tray positions if you are using two trays. The TURN FOOD notice appears only on AIR FRY and ROAST Smart Programs. If ROTATE is turned on, the message will not appear. Some food items do not need to be turned. Cooking will resume after 10 seconds, whether food has been turned or not.

- The display counts down the last cooking minute in seconds. When cooking is complete, you will hear a long beep and see a message on the display panel indicating END. If you leave food in the cooking chamber after the cooking is complete and the door is not opened, you will hear oven beeps to remind you that the food is ready. This occurs in 5-, 30- and 60-minute increments after the Smart Program ends.

- The oven will be hot during and after cooking, so always use proper hand protection when moving and removing cooking trays. Allow the oven to cool to room temperature before cleaning. Refer to the Care and Cleaning information in the user manual for proper cleaning actions and products.

THE PROGRAMS

AIR FRY: Use for all your favorite deep-fried meals, including fries, cauliflower wings, chicken nuggets and breaded sticks.

ROAST: This is ideal for beef, pork, lamb, poultry and vegetables.

BROIL: Use for top-down browned finishes on dishes such as nachos.

BAKE: Yes, you can bake cakes, brownies, cookies and one-dish, one-pan meals.

REHEAT: Reheat leftovers without overcooking or drying out.

DEHYDRATE: This is perfect for making fruit leathers, jerky or dried fruits and vegetables.

ROTISSERIE: Use for even all-over cooking, such as potatoes, and self-basting, such as chicken and other roasts.

PROOF: Allow your yeast doughs to rest and rise for light, airy loaves and breads.

TOAST: Use for golden finishes on breads and rolls.

SMART PROGRAMS

SMART FEATURES	DEFAULT TIME	TIME RANGE	DEFAULT TEMPERATURE	TEMPERATURE RANGE
AIR FRY	18 minutes	1 to 60 minutes	400°F (200°C)	180°F to 400°F (80°C to 200°C)
ROAST	40 minutes	1 to 60 minutes	380°F (193°C)	180°F to 400°F (80°C to 200°C)
BROIL	8 minutes	1 to 20 minutes	400°F (200°C)	400°F (200°C)
BAKE	30 minutes	1 to 60 minutes	365°F (185°C)	180°F to 400F (80°C to 200°C)
REHEAT	10 minutes	1 to 60 minutes	280°F (138°C)	120°F to 360°F (50°C to 182°C)
DEHYDRATE	7 hours	1 to 15 hours	120°F (50°C)	105°F to 160°F (40°C to 71°C)
PROOF	30 minutes	30 to 40 minutes	90°F (32°C)	90°F to 120°F (32°C to 50°C)

TOAST SMART PROGRAM (VORTEX PRO)

TOAST DARKNESS	DEFAULT TIME
Level 1	2:50 minutes
Level 2	3:10 minutes
Level 3	3:30 minutes

DONENESS OF FOOD

Always use a meat thermometer to check that your food has reached the safe minimum internal temperature. Many of the recipes in this book give the suggested internal temperature, but for further information, refer to the USDA's Safe Minimum Internal Temperature or Health Canada's Safe Internal Cooking Temperatures.

USING THE ROTISSERIE AND ACCESSORIES

The Instant Vortex Pro/Plus is equipped with One-Step Even Crisp Technology™ for simple rotisserie cooking with delicious results. The rotisserie is ideal for cooking whole roasts of chicken, beef, lamb and pork; it creates meat that is juicier because it is slow roasted and self-bastes as it rotates. Here are some more tips for successful rotisserie cooking.

- Always insert rotisserie accessories and food items into the cooking chamber before heating the oven.

- In using the rotisserie, always remember balance and safety. The maximum weight you can put on the Vortex spit is about 4 to 4½ lbs (2 to 2.25 kg). Anything larger will mean the food is not able to rotate freely and it may make contact with the heating coil — which could lead to fire and/or personal injury.

- When cooking poultry on the spit, ensure wings and legs are tied firmly with kitchen string.

- When using the rotisserie basket, do not overfill the basket. Overfilling may cause food to contact the heating elements, which may result in fire and/or personal injury.

- The Vortex Pro comes with a rotisserie lift, a handy tool that allows you to easily lift and slide the rotisserie basket and the spit into the oven. Do not try to lift and slide the basket or spit by hand — always use the lift. Refer to your Product, Parts and Accessories information in the User Manual for more detailed visual descriptions if needed.

ADDITIONAL ACCESSORIES

Besides the rotisserie basket and a rotisserie spit with attachments, your Instant Vortex Pro comes equipped with one drip pan and two cooking trays. There are three positions for the cooking trays: a top, middle and bottom position. The drip pan slides right into the very bottom of the oven (which is not the same as the bottom position) to assist in keeping the oven clean.

A few additional accessories were used to make some of the recipes in this book. Here are some you may wish to consider:

RAMEKINS: Small ramekins are great for making mini cakes and quiches. If they are oven safe, they are safe to use in the Vortex Pro. Four 6-oz (175 mL) size ramekins fit on one cooking tray.

SILICONE MUFFIN CUPS: These are oven safe and great for making mini meatloaves, muffins, egg cups and on-the-go frittatas.

CAKE PAN: An 8-inch (20 cm) round or 8- by 8-inch (20 by 20 cm) square metal pan, without handles, is perfect for making cinnamon rolls, cakes and brownies.

LOAF PAN: An 8- by 4-inch (20 by 10 cm) metal pan is ideal for making banana bread and other quick breads in the Vortex.

Also, I found that the best way to ensure these additional accessories lie flat in the Vortex oven is to flip the drip pan or a cooking tray over so that the raised side is facing up. (The only other time the drip pan is used, other than to protect the bottom of the oven, is when you would use it to cook something like granola, which needs a solid tray.)

PROTECT YOUR HANDS WHEN MOVING ACCESSORIES

Because the oven will be hot during and after cooking, you must always use proper hand protection to avoid burning your hands when you remove anything from the Vortex. You will want these useful tools to help you safely remove items from the Vortex:

TONGS: Wooden, metal or silicone-tipped tongs will allow you to safely remove pans that don't have handles. They will also help you flip food items when it is recommended to do so.

OVEN MITTS: Because of the tight oven space, it is sometimes challenging to use thick oven mitts to grab and grip cooking trays or accessories. Heat-resistant mini mitts or pinch mitts are small, food-grade silicone oven mitts that will easily allow you to slide cooking trays or lift pans from the cooking chamber.

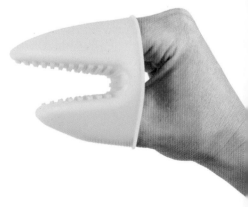

BREAKFASTS

BEST BANANA BREAD

MAKES 1 LOAF

Everyone has a favorite banana bread recipe. This is mine. It's a simple bread that relies on the flavor of the bananas. Mix it all easily by hand, or if you have a handheld or countertop electric mixer, use it to blend the butter and sugar.

PREP TIME
15 minutes

COOK TIME
40 minutes

VORTEX PROGRAM
▶ Bake

1½ cups (375 mL) all-purpose flour

½ tsp (2 mL) salt

½ cup (125 mL) butter

1 cup (250 mL) granulated sugar

2 ripe bananas, mashed (about ¾ cup/175 mL)

1 tsp (5 mL) baking soda

2 tbsp (30 mL) hot water

▶ HANDHELD OR STAND ELECTRIC MIXER (OPTIONAL)

▶ 8- BY 4-INCH (20 BY 10 CM) LOAF PAN

▶ WIRE COOLING RACK

1 Lightly grease an 8- by 4-inch (20 by 10 cm) loaf pan.

2 In a bowl, lightly sift together flour and salt; set aside.

3 In a separate bowl, blend together butter and sugar until light and fluffy with a spoon, or using an electric mixer if desired. Add bananas and stir until smooth.

4 In a measuring cup, dissolve baking soda in hot water; add to the banana mixture and stir until combined. Add flour mixture and gently stir by hand until mixture is just combined. Spoon mixture into prepared pan, smoothing out the top.

5 Place the drip pan or cooking tray in the bottom rack position (not the very bottom of the cooking chamber, where the drip pan usually goes), turned upside down so that the loaf pan will have a flat place to sit on. Using the display panel, select **BAKE**, set **TEMPERATURE** to 325°F (160°C) and set **TIME** to 40 minutes. **PREHEAT** Vortex until the display indicates **ADD FOOD**.

6 **BAKE** until banana bread is golden brown and a tester inserted in center comes out clean. Let pan cool on wire rack for 15 minutes. Run knife around edge; turn out loaf and let cool on wire rack.

TIPS Mixing the baking soda with boiling hot water ensures the soda is entirely dissolved and, when it reacts with the bananas, it creates a lighter textured quick bread.

The best bananas to use for banana bread are very ripe or overly ripe. If you have no time to bake when they are ripe, simply freeze whole bananas with the peel, then leave them to defrost at room temperature when you are ready. Or peel and mash bananas, then put them into containers and freeze for up to 2 months. Frozen banana purée may darken slightly but that will not affect the delicious baked results.

SUNDAY MORNING BREAKFAST POTATOES

MAKES 4 SERVINGS

There is very little wrong in life that can't be cured with potatoes — especially on a Sunday morning with fried eggs and freshly brewed coffee. These home fries, prepared with very little oil, are perfectly crispy. I prefer the skins on, but peel the potatoes if you are so inclined.

PREP TIME
10 minutes

COOK TIME
30 minutes

VORTEX PROGRAMS
▶ **Air Fry**
▶ **Rotate**

---

3 to 4 medium red potatoes (about 1 lb/500 g), skin on, cut into ½-inch (1 cm) cubes

1 medium onion, sliced

1 red bell pepper, chopped

1 tsp (5 mL) salt

½ tsp (2 mL) freshly ground black pepper

½ tsp (2 mL) smoked paprika

1 tbsp (15 mL) olive oil

▶ ROTISSERIE BASKET AND LIFT

1 In a large bowl, combine potatoes, onion slices, bell pepper, salt, pepper, paprika and oil; stir to combine and ensure the spices have completely coated the vegetables.

2 Place the drip pan in the bottom of the cooking chamber. Transfer vegetables to the rotisserie basket and secure lid in place. Using the rotisserie lift, lift the basket into the cooking chamber and slide the basket spit along the side bars until spit reaches the rotisserie hole. Pull forward on the red release lever to secure the ends of the basket spit in place.

3 Using the display panel, select **AIR FRY** and **ROTATE**, adjust **TEMPERATURE** to 350°F (180°C) and set **TIME** to 30 minutes. Press **START**. Cook until potatoes are golden brown and tender inside.

4 When unit finishes cooking, use rotisserie lift to remove basket, pulling forward on the red release lever to remove basket spit. Use oven mitts to remove lid. Serve hot.

TIPS Nowadays you can find smoked paprika in the spice section of most grocery stores. It generally comes in a sweet or hot version. If you like your potatoes with a little more kick, try the hot style. If you can't find smoked paprika, substitute regular paprika.

FRENCH TOAST
WITH SPICED MAPLE SYRUP

MAKES 2 SERVINGS

Crispy on the outside, soft and hot on the inside, this simple French Toast recipe makes a quick and delicious breakfast.

PREP TIME
5 minutes

COOK TIME
9 minutes

VORTEX PROGRAM
▶ **Air Fry**

FRENCH TOAST

1 tsp (5 mL) granulated sugar

½ tsp (2 mL) ground cinnamon

2 eggs, lightly beaten

⅓ cup (150 mL) milk

1 tsp (5 mL) vanilla

4 slices day-old bread

Olive oil cooking spray

SPICED MAPLE SYRUP

⅓ cup (75 mL) maple syrup

½ tsp (2 mL) ground cinnamon

½ tsp (2 mL) ground ginger

¼ tsp (1 mL) ground nutmeg

1 In a small bowl, blend sugar and cinnamon. Transfer to a sugar shaker or small sieve.

2 In a bowl, beat together eggs, milk and vanilla. Soak bread in egg mixture and lay out on cooking trays. Sprinkle sugar mixture over both sides of dipped bread slices. Lightly spray bread slices with cooking spray on one side.

3 Place drip pan in the bottom of the cooking chamber. Using the display panel, select **AIR FRY**, set **TEMPERATURE** to 370°F (185°C) and set **TIME** to 12 minutes. **PREHEAT** Vortex until display indicates **ADD FOOD**.

4 Slide cooking trays into the middle and bottom positions. When Vortex indicates **TURN FOOD**, turn bread slices over, spray other side with cooking spray and slide cooking tray that was in bottom position to top position and tray that was in middle position into bottom position.

5 Cook until toast is golden on both sides. Serve with Spiced Maple Syrup.

6 *Spiced Maple Syrup:* In a small pot, combine maple syrup, cinnamon, ginger and nutmeg and stir over medium heat until warm. Serve over French Toast.

TIPS Make sure you soak bread slices in egg mixture. Don't just dip them. You want the eggy goodness to soak into the bread completely.

I like to use a heartier type of bread, like a light rye or sourdough.

This French Toast recipe doubles easily, so you can freeze cooked slices for a quick grab-and-go breakfast. Place frozen bread slices on cooking trays and select **REHEAT**. Cook for 5 to 6 minutes until bread slices are hot.

Freeze uncooked slices in a single layer on a baking sheet lined with plastic wrap. When frozen, transfer to a sealable freezer bag and return to freezer. There is no need to defrost before cooking; reheat as directed in recipe, increasing cooking time by 5 minutes.

HAM & SWISS SOUFFLÉ EGG CUPS

MAKES 4 TO 6 SERVINGS

These easy, healthy egg "muffins" are a quick and flavorful low-carb breakfast that you can enjoy at home or as a morning snack you can easily bring to work. When they cook, they puff up just like a soufflé.

PREP TIME
10 minutes

COOK TIME
10 minutes

VORTEX PROGRAM
▶ Bake

7 large eggs

½ tsp (2 mL) salt

¼ tsp (1 mL) freshly ground black pepper

1 cup (250 mL) finely chopped ham

1 cup (250 mL) finely chopped baby spinach

1 cup (500 mL) grated Swiss cheese

½ cup (125 mL) chopped green onions, white and green parts

Hot sauce (optional)

▶ 12 SILICONE MUFFIN CUPS

1 In a blender or by hand, beat eggs with salt and pepper; set aside.

2 Set silicone cups around the outside edges of both cooking trays. Into each silicone muffin cup, evenly divide chopped ham, spinach, cheese and green onions. Add a dash of hot sauce, if desired. Evenly pour egg mixture over top of meat mixture, filling three-quarters of the way, ensuring cups don't overflow.

3 Place drip pan in the bottom of the cooking chamber. Using the display panel, select **BAKE**, then adjust **TEMPERATURE** to 400°F (200°C) and set **TIME** to 10 minutes. **PREHEAT** Vortex until display panel indicates **ADD FOOD**.

4 Slide cooking trays into top and bottom positions. When display indicates **TURN FOOD**, switch trays, moving bottom tray to top position and top tray to bottom position.

5 Remove soufflés from silicone cups before serving. Serve with additional hot sauce, if desired.

TIP To store any extra soufflé cups, remove from silicone cups and place in a sealed container in the refrigerator. To reheat, place soufflés directly on cooking trays. On the display panel, select **REHEAT**, then set **TEMPERATURE** to 300°F (150°C) and set **TIME** for 5 minutes.

VARIATIONS Feel free to add your own favorite fillings, such as chopped peppers, onions or cooked sausage.

BLUEBERRY LEMON BUTTERMILK MUFFINS

MAKES: 12 MUFFINS

A pot of coffee, a basket of muffins and a jar of honey — there is no better way to start the day.

PREP TIME
10 minutes

COOK TIME
20 minutes

VORTEX PROGRAM
▸ Bake

---

2 cups (500 mL)
all-purpose flour

2 tsp (10 mL) baking
powder

¼ tsp (1 mL) salt

½ cup (125 mL) softened
butter

1 cup (250 mL) granulated
sugar

2 eggs

Zest of 2 lemons

¾ cup (175 mL) buttermilk

1 cup (250 mL) fresh or
frozen blueberries

▸ 12 SILICONE MUFFIN CUPS

1 In a bowl, combine flour, baking powder and salt. In a separate bowl, cream butter with sugar; beat in eggs one at a time. Stir in lemon zest and buttermilk.

2 Make a well in the center of dry ingredients; pour in buttermilk mixture. Gently stir in blueberries just until incorporated.

3 Spoon into 12 silicone muffin cups. Place muffin cups on two cooking trays, around the outside (so the center is empty).

4 Using the display panel, select **BAKE**, adjust **TEMPERATURE** to 350°F (180°C) and set **TIME** to 20 minutes. **PREHEAT** Vortex until display indicates **ADD FOOD**.

5 Slide one cooking tray into middle position and bake until muffins are golden brown on top and firm to the touch. Let cool 5 minutes before transferring to a wire rack and cool completely. Repeat with the second tray of muffins.

TIPS Bake one tray at a time for best results, but this recipe can easily be cut in half in order to bake just six muffins.

Concerned about purchasing buttermilk and then only using a small amount? Use the rest to make the Best Buttermilk-Brined Fried Chicken (page 100) or substitute by placing 1 tbsp (15 mL) white vinegar or lemon juice in a measuring cup and adding enough milk to measure 1 cup (250 mL). Gently stir and let stand for 5 minutes before using.

Blueberries range in size from small flavorful wild berries to larger cultivated berries. You can use fresh or frozen for this recipe, but be careful when using frozen to only stir just until they are mixed in so that you don't turn your batter completely "blue."

MAPLE TURKEY BREAKFAST PATTIES

MAKES 4 SERVINGS

These delicious breakfast patties pair perfectly with a batch of fluffy homemade pancakes or my French Toast with Spiced Maple Syrup (see page 20).

PREP TIME
5 minutes

COOK TIME
8 minutes

VORTEX PROGRAM
▶ Air Fry

1 lb (500 g) lean ground turkey

2 tbsp (30 mL) maple syrup

1 tbsp (15 mL) dry barbecue seasoning mix, store-bought or homemade (see below)

Nonstick cooking spray

1 In a bowl, combine ground turkey, maple syrup and seasoning mix. With your hands, work the meat to form four patties, about 4 inches (10 cm) round, about 1/2 inch (1 cm) thick. Press a divot into the center of each patty on one side. (Patties can be refrigerated at this point for up to 24 hours for flavors to develop.)

2 Using the display panel, select **AIR FRY**, adjust **TEMPERATURE** to 375°F (190°C) and set **TIME** to 8 minutes. **PREHEAT** Vortex until display indicates **ADD FOOD**.

3 Spray patties lightly with cooking spray. Place patties divot side down on two cooking trays. Place cooking trays in bottom and middle positions. When display indicates **TURN FOOD**, switch bottom cooking tray to top position and middle cooking tray to bottom position.

4 Cook until patties are golden brown and internal cooked temperature indicates 165°F (74°C) when measured with a meat thermometer.

TIP To cook one to two patties, place on cooking tray and slide into middle position of cooking chamber. Cook as directed above.

DRY BARBECUE SEASONING MIX
MAKES 3⅓ TBSP (49 ML)

Many factors go into how long spices will last, including temperature, humidity and the freshness of the ingredients you are using. While you can use a prepared barbecue seasoning mix, I often make this one up in the summer and use it for lots of different recipes.

1 tbsp (15 mL) smoked paprika, sweet or hot

2 tsp (10 mL) brown sugar

1 tsp (5 mL) celery salt

1 tsp (5 mL) garlic powder

1 tsp (5 mL) dry mustard

1½ tsp (7 mL) salt

½ tsp (2 mL) freshly ground black pepper

1 Mix all ingredients in a bowl and store in an airtight jar for up to 2 months.

"THESE DELICIOUS BREAKFAST PATTIES PAIR PERFECTLY WITH A BATCH OF FLUFFY HOMEMADE PANCAKES."

NUTTY PUMPKIN PIE GRANOLA

MAKES 4 CUPS (1 L)

This recipe packs plenty of punch in healthy fats, omega-3s and protein from nuts and seeds. Naturally sweetened with honey and peanut butter, it's nice and crunchy on its own, but I like to add a few cranberries or raisins for extra sweetness.

PREP TIME
15 minutes

COOK TIME
20 to 25 minutes

VORTEX PROGRAM
▶ Bake

2 cups (500 mL) quick oats

½ cup (125 mL) chopped nuts (walnuts, almonds, pecans)

¼ cup (60 mL) unsweetened coconut

¼ cup (60 mL) pumpkin seeds

2 tbsp (30 mL) each sunflower, sesame and whole flax seeds

½ cup (125 mL) liquid honey or maple syrup

¼ cup (60 mL) peanut butter or other nut butter

½ tsp (2 mL) salt

¼ tsp (1 mL) pumpkin pie spice or ground cinnamon

▶ ALUMINUM FOIL

1 Line cooking trays with aluminum foil, wrapping it around the edges.

2 In a large bowl, combine oats, nuts, coconut, and pumpkin, sunflower, sesame and flax seeds; set aside.

3 In another bowl or measure, combine honey, peanut butter, salt and pumpkin pie spice; stir together until completely blended, then pour over oat mixture. Mix well, ensuring everything has been coated with honey mixture, and turn out onto prepared cooking trays.

4 Using the display panel, select **BAKE**, then adjust **TEMPERATURE** to 275°F (140°C) and set **TIME** to 20 minutes. Select **START** to preheat.

5 When Vortex displays **ADD FOOD**, slide cooking trays into top and bottom positions.

6 When display panel indicates **TURN FOOD**, remove cooking trays. Stir granola on each tray, then place tray that was in top position into the bottom position and tray that was in bottom position into top position.

7 When cooked, remove trays and allow mixture to cool completely. Store granola in an airtight container for up to 1 month.

TIPS Eat this granola with your favorite milk or dairy-free beverage or yogurt. If you are like me and can't kick cereal altogether, it makes a great addition to bran flakes to bulk up the protein content.

For a vegan option, use maple syrup instead of honey.

Customize the nuts and seeds to use whatever you have on hand.

Stir the granola every 7 minutes just to ensure the top tray doesn't get too brown.

RED PEPPER & PANCETTA FRITTATA

SERVES 4 TO 6

Nothing beats a delicious egg dish like this frittata for a special occasion brunch or an easy supper dish. A frittata is an Italian version of an omelet. Unlike its finicky cousin, which needs careful tending, a frittata requires no special cooking skills other than stirring — so it's almost impossible to ruin.

PREP TIME

15 minutes

COOK TIME

25 minutes

VORTEX PROGRAMS

▸ **Air Fry**

▸ **Bake**

---

1 red bell pepper, diced

1 onion, diced

6 slices pancetta

Olive oil cooking spray

2 small potatoes, cooked

1 tbsp (15 mL) finely chopped fresh oregano (or 1 tsp/5 mL dried)

1 tbsp (15 mL) finely chopped fresh rosemary (or 1 tsp/5 mL dried)

6 eggs

1 tbsp (15 mL) Dijon mustard

¼ cup (60 mL) milk or cream

1 tsp (5 mL) salt

½ tsp (2 mL) freshly ground black pepper

½ cup (125 mL) crumbled feta or goat's cheese

▸ PARCHMENT PAPER

▸ 8-INCH (20 CM) ROUND OR 8- BY 8-INCH (20 BY 20 CM) SQUARE NONSTICK BAKING PAN

1 Crumble a piece of parchment paper into a small ball, then run it under warm water, gently squeezing parchment until it begins to soften. Once softened, squeeze all excess water out of paper, then straighten it and line baking pan with dampened paper. Parchment will hang over edges of pan.

2 Place bell pepper, onion and pancetta in baking pan and spray lightly with cooking spray.

3 Using the display panel, select **AIR FRY**, set **TEMPERATURE** to 400°F (200°C) and set **TIME** to 10 minutes. **PREHEAT** Vortex until display indicates **ADD FOOD**.

4 Turn drip pan upside down and slide into bottom position of the cooking chamber. Set baking pan on top of drip pan. Close door and cook until display indicates **TURN FOOD**.

5 Stir onion mixture and continue to cook until onions have softened and pancetta is slightly crisped.

6 Remove baking pan, cooling for 5 minutes. Add potatoes, oregano and rosemary; stir to combine.

7 Meanwhile, in a bowl combine eggs, mustard, milk, salt and pepper. Pour mixture over vegetables and sprinkle with cheese; stir so that all ingredients are completely covered with egg mixture.

8 Using the display panel, select **BAKE**, set **TEMPERATURE** to 325°F (160°C) and set **TIME** to 25 minutes. **PREHEAT** Vortex until display indicates **ADD FOOD**.

9 Add baking pan and cook until golden brown on top and eggs are just set in the center. Let cool 5 minutes. Lift out parchment paper from pan, peel away sides and cut into wedges or squares.

TIP This is a perfect dish to use up any leftover potatoes.

SMOKED MEAT & SWISS TURNOVERS

MAKES 8 TURNOVERS

I stumbled across these handheld packages when I was visiting a quaint bakery near Peggy's Cove, Nova Scotia. My friend Karen and I each ordered one, then I stood and watched the baker make them. There are only three ingredients — mustard, smoked meat and Swiss cheese — but that doesn't make it any less tasty.

PREP TIME
15 minutes

COOK TIME
20 minutes

VORTEX PROGRAM
▸ **Air Fry**

---

1 package (1 lb / 500 g) puff pastry sheets, each sheet cut into four 12- by 4-inch (30 by 10 cm) strips

¼ cup (60 mL) grainy mustard

8 slices Montreal smoked meat

8 slices Swiss cheese, each cut into 4- by 2-inch (10 by 5 cm) rectangles

1 egg, lightly beaten

▸ PASTRY BRUSH

1 Cut puff pastry sheets into eight strips and lay out on cutting board.

2 On the bottom half of the strip spread 1 tbsp (15 mL) grainy mustard. Lay one piece of cheese on top of mustard, then one slice smoked meat on top of cheese and finish with one piece of cheese on top of meat.

3 With a pastry brush, brush three edges of pastry with egg wash. Fold the one half of the pastry over the other, with edges coming to meet. Using a fork, crimp the edges of the pastry on all sides to make an edge. Cut a small slit in the top of the pastry to let steam out. Repeat with three more pastry strips, laying two pastries on each cooking tray.

4 Place drip pan in the bottom of the cooking chamber. Using the display panel, select **AIR FRY**, set **TEMPERATURE** to 400°F (200°C) and set **TIME** to 15 minutes. **PREHEAT** Vortex until display indicates **ADD FOOD**.

5 Slide cooking trays into the bottom and top positions. When Vortex indicates **TURN FOOD**, turn pastries over and move tray that was in bottom position to top position and tray that was in top position to bottom position.

6 Continue to cook until pastries are golden and puffed.

TIP To thaw puff pastry, place in refrigerator overnight. Do not microwave. Keep refrigerated until ready to use.

HARD-COOKED EGGS
WITH EVERYTHING SPICE

MAKES 6

Making hard-"boiled" eggs in the Vortex is quick and easy and involves virtually no water except for after the cooking.

PREP TIME

5 minutes

COOK TIME

15 to 17 minutes

VORTEX PROGRAM

▶ Air Fry

EVERYTHING SPICE

2 tbsp (30 mL) poppy seeds

1 tbsp (15 mL) white sesame seeds

1 tbsp (15 mL) black sesame seeds

1 tbsp (15 mL) dried minced garlic

1 tbsp (15 mL) dried onion flakes

2 tsp (10 mL) flaked or coarse sea salt

HARD-COOKED EGGS

6 large eggs

1 *Everything Spice:* In a small bowl, combine poppy seeds, sesame seeds, dried garlic, onion flakes and salt. Stir until combined. Store in a sealed jar or container.

2 *Hard-Cooked Eggs:* Using the display panel, select **AIR FRY**, set **TEMPERATURE** to 250°F (120°C) and set **TIME** for 15 minutes (for softer yolk) or 17 minutes (for a firmer yolk). **PREHEAT** Vortex until display indicates **ADD FOOD**.

3 Place eggs on cooking tray and slide into middle position. When eggs are finished cooking, immediately transfer to a bowl of ice water. Let stand for 3 minutes before peeling.

4 Garnish with Everything Spice mixture.

TIPS Hard-cooked eggs peel much more easily when they are not super fresh. Eggs that have been sitting in your refrigerator for a few days are just right.

You can use this method of cooking eggs for my Crispy Deviled Eggs (page 35).

APPETIZERS

AVOCADO FRIES
WITH LIME SRIRACHA DIP

MAKES 2 TO 4 SERVINGS

A healthy appetizer or snack, these are sure to become your new addiction. While they are tasty on their own, it's the dipping sauce that ties the whole thing together. You can easily double this recipe if you have company.

PREP TIME
10 minutes

COOK TIME
8 minutes

VORTEX PROGRAM
▶ Air Fry

AVOCADO FRIES

1 medium avocado (or 2 small), peeled, pitted and sliced

½ tsp (2 mL) garlic powder

½ tsp (2 mL) salt

¼ cup (60 mL) chickpea flour (or all-purpose gluten-free flour)

½ cup (125 mL) orange juice

1 cup (250 mL) crushed sweet Thai chili corn chips

Nonstick cooking spray

LIME SRIRACHA DIP

¼ cup (60 mL) mayonnaise or vegan mayonnaise

2 tsp (10 mL) Thai chile sauce (such as Sriracha), or more to taste

1 clove garlic, minced

1 lime, juiced

1 *Avocado Fries:* Slice avocado into ¼-inch (0.5 cm) slices or about 12 slices.

2 In a bowl, combine garlic powder, salt and chickpea flour. Place orange juice in a second bowl and then the crushed corn chips in a third bowl.

3 Using a two-handed method, coat avocado slices first in seasoned flour mixture, then transfer to the orange juice and, using the other hand, dip the slices in the wet mixture. Transfer avocado slices to the corn chip bowl and coat both sides using a dry hand. Lay slices onto two cooking trays, leaving space around slices. Lightly spray slices with cooking spray.

4 Using the display panel, select **AIR FRY**, set **TEMPERATURE** to 400°F (200°C) and set **TIME** to 8 minutes. Press **START** to preheat.

5 When Vortex displays **ADD FOOD**, place one tray in the top position and the other tray in the bottom position.

6 **AIR FRY** until crispy, switching cooking trays when the display says **TURN FOOD** so the tray that was in the top position moves to the bottom position and the tray from the bottom moves to the top.

7 *Lime Sriracha Dip:* In a small bowl, mix together mayonnaise, Sriracha, garlic and lime juice. Serve fries warm with Lime Sriracha Dip

---

TIPS You want perfectly ripe avocados to make this snack. To know if an avocado is ready, check under the stem. If you peel back the small stem or cap at the top of the avocado and it comes away easily, you should find a nice creamy green center. If too ripe, it will be brown underneath the stem; if not ripe enough, the stem won't come off.

When you purchase avocados, the skin should be dark green to black and bumpy. The fruit should feel heavy and firm with no obvious soft parts or flat areas.

BACON-WRAPPED CHICKEN WINGS
WITH BEER SMEAR SAUCE

MAKES 4 TO 6 SERVINGS

Avoid Buffalo wing burnout and cook up a batch of these wings for your next get-together. The homemade beer barbecue sauce is made with pantry staples and a good dark beer, but you can use your favorite ready-made barbecue sauce instead. Have lots of napkins on hand for sticky fingers and saucy lips.

PREP TIME
15 minutes

COOK TIME
20 minutes

VORTEX PROGRAM
▶ Air Fry

BEER SMEAR SAUCE

2 cups (500 mL) ketchup

1 can (12 oz/341 mL) beer

2 tbsp (30 mL) apple cider vinegar

2 tbsp (30 mL) molasses

2 tbsp (30 mL) brown sugar

2 tbsp (30 mL) chili powder

2 tbsp (30 mL) yellow mustard

1 tsp (15 mL) smoked paprika

⅛ to ¼ tsp (0.5 to 1 mL) cayenne pepper

WINGS

1 lb (500 g) split chicken wings, wingettes and drumettes (about 16 pieces)

Salt and freshly ground black pepper

8 to 9 strips bacon, cut in half crosswise

1 *Beer Smear Sauce:* In a saucepan, whisk together ketchup, beer, vinegar, molasses, brown sugar, chili powder, mustard, smoked paprika and cayenne. Bring mixture to a boil over medium-high heat. Reduce heat and simmer 20 to 30 minutes until thickened and reduced. Taste and adjust seasonings.

2 *Bacon-Wrapped Chicken Wings:* Season chicken wings liberally with salt and pepper. Wrap each wingette and drumette with a half slice of bacon. Lay wrapped chicken wings on cooking trays, leaving a little space around each one to ensure they don't overlap.

3 Place the drip pan in the bottom of the cooking chamber. Using the display panel, select **AIR FRY**, set **TEMPERATURE** to 400°F (200°C) and set **TIME** to 15 minutes. **PREHEAT** Vortex until display indicates **ADD FOOD**.

4 Set cooking tray in the bottom and top positions. When display indicates **TURN FOOD**, turn the chicken wings over and switch cooking trays so tray in the bottom position moves to the top position and top tray moves to bottom position. Close door and continue to cook until chicken wings are golden brown, bacon is cooked and juices of chicken run clear when pierced with a knife.

5 Transfer to bowl and toss with ¼ cup (60 mL) Beer Smear Sauce. Serve warm with more sauce for dipping.

TIPS Purchase already split chicken wings in the fresh meat section of the grocery store. If you can't find them, split them yourself with a sharp knife between the joint. Discard the wing tip. You can use frozen split chicken wings, but you will need to thaw them first.

Store any leftover Beer Smear Sauce in a sealed jar in the refrigerator for up to 3 months.

CRISPY DEVILED EGGS

MAKES 4 SERVINGS

This recipe takes deviled eggs to a whole new level. The whites are crispy and crunchy and topped with a creamy yolk filling. You won't be able to stop at just one!

PREP TIME
25 minutes

COOK TIME
6 to 8 minutes

VORTEX PROGRAM
▶ Air Fry

6 large eggs (see Hard-Cooked Eggs, page 29)

3 tbsp (45 mL) mayonnaise

1 tbsp (15 mL) sour cream

1 tsp (5 mL) hot sauce

1 tsp (5 mL) Dijon mustard

½ tsp (2 mL) salt

¼ tsp (1 mL) freshly ground black pepper

½ cup (125 mL) all-purpose or gluten-free flour

1 tsp (5 mL) garlic powder

2 eggs, well beaten

¾ cup (175 mL) panko or gluten-free bread crumbs

Nonstick cooking spray

Chopped parsley

▶ PASTRY BAG (PIPING BAG) OR SEALABLE STORAGE BAG

1 Slice hard-cooked eggs in half lengthwise; remove yolks to a medium bowl and place egg whites on a plate. Mash egg yolks with a fork until crumbly.

2 To the yolks, add mayonnaise, sour cream, hot sauce, mustard, salt and pepper. Stir until well blended, then set aside.

3 Set up a dredging and dipping station with two plates and a bowl. In one bowl, combine flour and garlic powder. In a second bowl, beat eggs until well combined. Place panko in a third bowl.

4 Dip egg whites into seasoned flour, then transfer to beaten egg mixture to coat, and finally dip into panko, ensuring all sides and center of egg whites are coated with panko. Place eggs on two cooking trays, hollow side up. Do not crowd the eggs. Spray all over with cooking spray.

5 Place drip pan in the bottom of cooking chamber. Using the display panel, select **AIR FRY**, adjust **TEMPERATURE** to 380°F (193°C) and set **TIME** for 8 minutes.

6 When display indicates **ADD FOOD**, slide trays into top and bottom positions.

7 When display indicates **TURN FOOD**, switch the cooking trays around so that the tray in the top position moves to the bottom position and the tray in bottom position moves to the top position.

8 When cooking is finished, transfer eggs to a plate. Cool for 5 to 10 minutes before filling with yolk mixture. Garnish with chopped parsley.

TIPS Make a bag for piping from a sealable storage bag. Simply fill bag with egg yolk mixture, then snip off one of the corners with kitchen scissors and squeeze filling into egg white without making a huge mess.

These eggs transport wonderfully and stay crispy for a long time. Rather than pre-filling the eggs, pack whites into one container and yolk mixture into another. Fill just before serving.

BACON-WRAPPED CHEESE-STUFFED JALAPEÑOS

MAKES 4 TO 6 SERVINGS (GF)

I have a weakness for jalapeño poppers but would never deep fry them at home. The Vortex does a great job of air frying them and achieves a very similar result. This is the ultimate party or game-day snack!

PREP TIME
15 minutes

COOK TIME
17 minutes

VORTEX PROGRAM
▶ Air Fry

12 jalapeño peppers, about 3 to 4 inches (7.5 to 10 cm) long, cut in half, seeds and ribs removed

4 oz (125 g) cream cheese, softened

½ cup (125 mL) shredded Cheddar cheese

1 clove garlic, minced

2 green onions, white and green parts, finely chopped

½ tsp (2 mL) salt

½ tsp (2 mL) freshly ground black pepper

6 slices bacon, cut in half crosswise

1 Cut jalapeños in half lengthwise and use a sharp paring knife or spoon to scoop out the seeds and ribs.

2 In a bowl, combine softened cream cheese, Cheddar cheese, garlic, green onions, salt and pepper; blend well.

3 Using a small spoon or kitchen knife, fill each jalapeño half with cheese mixture. Wrap each jalapeño with slice of bacon, then place jalapeño stuffed side up on cooking tray. Continue until all jalapeños are filled, wrapped and placed on two cooking trays.

4 Place the drip pan in the bottom of the cooking chamber. Using the display panel, select **AIR FRY**, adjust **TEMPERATURE** to 400°F (200°C) and set **TIME** to 8 minutes. Press **START**. **PREHEAT** Vortex until display indicates **ADD FOOD**.

5 Slide one cooking tray into the bottom position and the other tray into the top position. When indicator signals **TURN FOOD**, switch cooking trays so the tray that was in the top position is now in the bottom position and the other tray moves to the top position. Continue to cook until the filling is golden and bubbling and bacon is crispy and browned.

6 Using a nonstick spatula, transfer poppers to a serving platter. Cool a few minutes before serving.

TIPS You don't want jalapeños that are too small; otherwise, they are too difficult to fill. Likewise, you don't want them too big.

Removing seeds and ribs from the jalapeños removes most of the heat from the pepper. If your hands are sensitive to pepper, use a pair of latex gloves for this step.

Don't use thick-cut bacon for this recipe; it is too difficult to wrap around the peppers. I like to use what I call "stretchy bacon."

BUFFALO CAULIFLOWER BITES
WITH BLUE CHEESE DIP

MAKES 4 SERVINGS

Savory, spicy, secretly healthy, surprisingly delicious. These six-ingredient cauliflower bites are perfect for game day, summer barbecue parties and potlucks, whenever you are craving seriously fun comfort food that won't leave you weighed down. Okay, there may be some die-hard meat eaters you won't convince, but I guarantee most people will gobble them up at lightning speed and then ask you for the recipe.

PREP TIME
20 minutes

COOK TIME
17 minutes

VORTEX PROGRAMS
▶ **Air Fry**
▶ **Rotate (optional)**
▶ **Reheat**

BUFFALO CAULIFLOWER WINGS

1 medium cauliflower, cut into florets (about 25 to 30)

½ cup (125 mL) all-purpose flour (or almond flour)

¼ tsp (1 mL) garlic powder

½ cup (125 mL) mayonnaise or vegan mayo

7 tbsp (105 mL) hot pepper sauce (such as Frank's RedHot sauce), divided

Oil spray

1 tbsp (15 mL) melted butter or vegan spread

continued →

▶ ROTISSERIE BASKET (OPTIONAL)

1 *Buffalo Cauliflower Wings:* Remove outer leaves and stem from cauliflower. Cut into florets, making sure there is a small stem to hold on to. Cut florets so there is a flat side. You should get about 25 to 30 florets from one cauliflower.

2 In a medium bowl, combine flour with garlic powder; set aside. In a separate bowl, combine mayonnaise with 1 tbsp (15 mL) hot pepper sauce, mixing well.

3 Using a two-handed method, dip cauliflower florets with one hand into mayonnaise mixture, letting excess drip off. Ensure all areas of cauliflower are coated and there are no bare spots. Transfer to flour mixture and, using the other hand, toss cauliflower in flour mixture (or almond flour, if using). Place florets in the rotisserie basket or on two cooking trays. Lightly spray with cooking spray.

4 Using the display panel, select **AIR FRY**, adjust **TEMPERATURE** to 380°F (193°C) and set **TIME** to 12 minutes.

5 *If using rotisserie basket:* Place the drip pan in the bottom of the cooking chamber. After the cauliflower is placed in the basket, secure the lid and lock into place. Using the rotisserie lift, lift the basket into the cooking chamber and slide the spit along the side bars until spit reaches the rotisserie hole. Pull forward on the red release lever to secure the ends of the spit in place. Close the door and select **ROTATE**. Press **START**. *If using cooking trays:* PREHEAT Vortex first according to cooking directions above. When display indicates **ADD FOOD**, insert one cooking tray into the top position and the other tray into the bottom position. Close the door.

BLUE CHEESE DIP

½ cup (125 mL)
mayonnaise or vegan mayo

¼ cup (60 mL) crumbled
blue cheese

6 While food is cooking, in a bowl, combine remaining 6 tbsp (90 mL) hot pepper sauce and melted butter. Stir to combine. Once cooking is complete, remove basket or trays from the cooking chamber.

7 Add cooked cauliflower to hot sauce mixture and toss to coat with sauce. Transfer onto cooking trays.

8 Using the display panel, select **REHEAT**, then adjust **TEMPERATURE** to 300°F (150°C). Press **START**. **PREHEAT** Vortex until display indicates **ADD FOOD**.

9 Place trays into the top and bottom position. Close the door. Using the display panel, set **TIME** for 5 minutes. When the program is complete, remove from cooking chamber, transfer to serving plate and serve immediately with Blue Cheese Dip.

10 *Blue Cheese Dip:* In a bowl, combine mayonnaise and crumbled cheese. Serve alongside cauliflower wings.

TIPS To make this gluten-free or keto-friendly, substitute ½ cup (125 mL) all-purpose flour with 1 cup (125 mL) almond flour.

Use a two-handed method to dredge or coat the cauliflower with mayonnaise and flour. With one hand, coat the cauliflower in mayonnaise and shake off any excess. Make sure there are no bare spots or areas where the mayonnaise mixture is bare. The hand you used will be your "wet hand." (If you use your left, you will proceed from left to right.) Transfer the cauliflower to the flour mixture, and use your other hand to coat. This will be your "dry hand." Try not to let the dry hand touch the wet mixture; otherwise, you'll make a big gooey mess.

CHEESY BLUE STUFFED MUSHROOMS

MAKES 4 TO 6 SERVINGS

GF

Everyone loves stuffed mushrooms. These little mouthfuls are puffy, perky and packed with cheesy flavor. Pre-baking the mushroom cups removes excess moisture. With so few ingredients, you can easily make a double batch. Leftovers — if you are so lucky — store well and reheat when you want a second helping.

PREP TIME
20 minutes

COOK TIME
10 minutes

VORTEX PROGRAMS
▶ **Air Fry**
▶ **Broil**

1 lb (500 g) mushrooms, medium sized, cleaned and stems removed

Nonstick cooking spray

4 oz (125 g) cream cheese, softened

¼ cup (60 mL) blue cheese, crumbled

2 green onions, white and green parts, finely chopped

Salt and freshly ground black pepper

1 Remove stems from the mushrooms and finely chop. Place chopped stems in the drip pan and lay mushroom caps on both cooking trays, cap side down. Lightly spray chopped stems and caps with cooking spray.

2 Meanwhile in a bowl, combine cream cheese, blue cheese and green onions. Season to taste with salt and pepper; set aside.

3 Using the display panel, select **AIR FRY**, set **TEMPERATURE** to 400°F (200°C) and set **TIME** to 5 minutes. **PREHEAT** Vortex until display indicates **ADD FOOD**.

4 Slide drip pan onto the bottom of the cooking chamber, and the cooking trays into the bottom and top cooking positions. Close door and cook until display indicates **TURN FOOD**.

5 Transfer bottom tray to top position and top to bottom position. Continue to cook until mushrooms have released their moisture.

6 Remove all the cooking trays from the cooking chamber. Add cooked stems to cheese mixture and stir until combined. Turn mushroom caps over and, using a paper towel, soak up excess water pooled inside them.

7 Using a teaspoon, fill mushroom caps and place all mushrooms onto one cooking tray. Using the display panel, select **BROIL**, set **TEMPERATURE** to 400°F (200°C) and set **TIME** to 5 minutes. When display indicates **ADD FOOD**, slide cooking tray into middle position.

8 **BROIL** until tops of mushrooms are golden brown and bubbling.

TIPS These mushrooms can be made ahead. Prepare without broiling, then freeze mushrooms in a single layer on a baking sheet. When frozen, pack into sealable freezer bags. When ready to cook, place frozen mushrooms on cooking tray. Using the display panel, select **REHEAT**, set **TEMPERATURE** to 300°F (150°C) and set **TIME** to 8 minutes. When display indicates **ADD FOOD**, slide cooking tray into middle rack position. Cook until mushrooms are warmed through. Continue with Broil as recipe indicates in Step 7, left.

VARIATIONS You can substitute sharp (old) Cheddar cheese for blue cheese. For an added crunch, add 1 tbsp (15 mL) crumbled cooked bacon to the cheese mixture.

"THESE LITTLE MOUTHFULS ARE PUFFY, PERKY AND PACKED WITH CHEESY FLAVOR."

COCONUT SHRIMP
WITH MANGO CURRY AÏOLI

MAKES 4 SERVINGS

A shot of hot sauce in the batter counters the sweetness of the shrimp, which get a double dose of crunch from a coating of shredded coconut and panko.

PREP TIME
20 minutes

COOK TIME
10 minutes

VORTEX PROGRAMS
▶ Air Fry

MANGO CURRY AÏOLI

1/2 cup (125 mL) mango chutney

1 cup (250 mL) mayonnaise

1/2 tsp (2 mL) curry powder

1/2 tsp (2 mL) salt

SHRIMP

1/2 cup (125 mL) all-purpose flour

1 tbsp (15 mL) granulated sugar

1 tbsp (15 mL) seafood seasoning (such as Old Bay)

Salt

1/2 cup (125 mL) pale lager beer (such as Corona)

2 tbsp (30 mL) hot pepper sauce (such as Frank's RedHot sauce)

continued →

1 *Mango Curry Aïoli:* In a bowl, combine chutney, mayonnaise, curry powder and salt. Mix well and set aside.

2 *Coconut Shrimp:* In a medium bowl, whisk together flour, sugar, seafood seasoning and 1/2 tsp (2 mL) salt; then slowly whisk in the beer and hot sauce to make a smooth batter. In a shallow bowl, combine the panko and shredded coconut.

3 Holding a shrimp by its tail, dip it into the batter, letting any excess drip off, then dredge it in the panko mixture, pressing and rolling it several times to coat well. Transfer to cooking trays, giving space around each shrimp so they don't overlap. Spray shrimp evenly with cooking spray.

4 Place the drip pan in the bottom of the cooking chamber. Using display panel, select **AIR FRY**, set **TEMPERATURE** to 400°F (200°C) and set **TIME** to 10 minutes. **PREHEAT** Vortex until display indicates **ADD FOOD**.

5 Slide cooking trays into middle and bottom positions and close door. When display indicates **TURN FOOD**, turn shrimp over on each cooking tray and switch bottom tray to top position and middle tray to bottom position. Cook until shrimp are pink and crust is golden. Serve the shrimp with the Mango Curry Aïoli.

TIPS Make sure to use unsweetened coconut on these shrimps. Using sweetened coconut will result in a burned crust on the shrimp.

Shrimp are sold by the pound, and the size on the package indicates how many you get per pound. I like to use the colossal (13 to 15) or jumbo (21 to 25) size to make coconut shrimp that have the shells on. That way I can easily peel them down to the tail, and use the tail to hang on to when dipping into the batter.

½ cup (125 mL) panko bread crumbs

½ cup (125 mL) unsweetened shredded coconut

12 large (13 to 15 per lb) shrimp, peeled and deveined, tails intact

Coconut oil cooking spray

To thaw frozen shrimp, put them in a bowl in the refrigerator or, for faster results, take them out of the package and put in a bowl of cold water and let a trickle of water run into the bowl while excess water goes down the drain. The shrimp should be ready in about 15 minutes. Let dry on paper towel–lined tray before dipping.

VARIATION To make gluten free, substitute gluten-free all-purpose flour and panko bread crumbs for regular flour and bread crumbs. Replace beer with a gluten-free option or sparkling water or ginger ale.

FULLY LOADED JALAPEÑO POTATOES

SERVES 2 TO 4   (GF)

Homemade potato skins are one of my son Jack's absolute favorite appetizers. He was happy to act as official taste tester for this recipe and quite particular about the filling. We made them savory with a garlicky exterior and fully loaded with a bacon, cheese and green onion stuffing on the top.

PREP TIME
10 minutes

COOK TIME
35 minutes

VORTEX PROGRAMS
▶ Air Fry
▶ Bake

FILLING

2 green onions, whites and green parts, finely chopped

1 small jalapeño pepper (or ½ large), seeded and finely chopped

1 cup (250 mL) shredded Cheddar cheese

2 slices cooked bacon, chopped (optional)

¼ cup (60 mL) sour cream

FULLY LOADED JALAPEÑO POTATOES

2 medium russet potatoes, scrubbed

Nonstick cooking spray

Salt and freshly ground black pepper

Garlic powder

Chopped chives

Sour cream (optional)

1 *Filling:* In a bowl, combine green onions, jalapeño, cheese, bacon (if using) and sour cream; mix well and set aside.

2 *Fully Loaded Jalapeño Potatoes:* Cut russet potatoes in half lengthwise. Spray each half of potatoes all over with cooking spray. Season with salt, pepper and garlic powder on all sides, then lay on cooking trays, cut side down.

3 Place the drip pan in the bottom of the cooking chamber. Using display panel, select **AIR FRY**, set **TEMPERATURE** to 380°F (193°C) and set **TIME** to 30 minutes. **PREHEAT** Vortex until display indicates **ADD FOOD**.

4 Slide cooking trays into top and bottom positions and close door. When display indicates **TURN FOOD**, turn potatoes over on each cooking tray and switch bottom tray to top position and top tray to bottom position. Cook until potatoes are golden brown and flesh is tender when pierced with a knife. Allow potatoes to cool for 5 minutes. Transfer the four potatoes onto one tray.

5 Top each potato with one-quarter of the filling mixture. Select **BAKE** on display panel, set **TEMPERATURE** to 400°F (200°C) and set **TIME** for 5 minutes. **PREHEAT** Vortex until display indicates **ADD FOOD**. Slide cooking tray into middle position. Cook until cheese is melted and topping is bubbly.

6 Garnish with chives and serve with additional sour cream if using.

TIP Russets are the best potatoes for this recipe. They have the fluffy, starchy texture that is essential in a baked potato.

VARIATIONS There are lots of ways to top these potato skins. Mix taco-seasoned ground beef or turkey with shredded Cheddar and chopped fresh cilantro. Or try leftover pulled pork.

GINGER-GLAZED COCKTAIL RIBLETS

MAKES 4 SERVINGS

These cocktail ribs are the ideal finger food. Adding water into the drip pan in the bottom of cooking chamber helps to keep the meat tender as it roasts. You can use either back or spare ribs, but I find the back ribs a little meatier. As they cook, the meat pulls away from the bone, creating a convenient handle for picking them up.

PREP TIME

10 minutes

COOK TIME

25 minutes

VORTEX PROGRAMS

▶ **Roast**

▶ **Rotate**

▶ **Bake**

GINGER-GLAZED COCKTAIL RIBLETS

2½ lbs (1.25 kg) meaty pork loin baby back or spare ribs, cut into individual single rib portions

Salt and freshly ground black pepper

GINGER GLAZE

⅓ cup (75 mL) chili sauce

¼ cup (60 mL) apricot jam

1 tbsp (15 mL) finely chopped gingerroot (or 1 tsp/5 mL ground ginger)

Chopped green onions

▶ ROTISSERIE BASKET AND LIFT

1 *Ginger-Glazed Cocktail Riblets:* Cut ribs into single rib portions. Season well on all sides with salt and pepper. Place riblets in rotisserie basket and secure lid.

2 Place drip pan in the bottom of the cooking chamber. Pour 1 cup (250 mL) of water into the bottom of the drip pan.

3 Using the rotisserie lift, slide the rotisserie basket along the side bars until it reaches the rotisserie hole. Pull forward to the red release lever to secure the ends of the basket in place. Close the door.

4 Using the display panel, select **ROAST** and **ROTATE**, adjust **TEMPERATURE** to 350°F (180°C) and set **TIME** for 25 minutes, then select **START**.

5 *Ginger Glaze:* While meat is cooking, in a large bowl, combine chili sauce, apricot jam and ginger; set aside until riblets are cooked.

6 Remove basket from cooking chamber by pulling forward on the red release lever and lifting out using the rotisserie lift. Allow basket to cool for 5 minutes before removing lid. Transfer riblets to sauce bowl and toss in sauce to coat.

7 Lay coated riblets on cooking tray. Using display panel, select **BAKE**, set **TEMPERATURE** to 300°F and set **TIME** to 8 minutes. **PREHEAT** Vortex until display indicates **ADD FOOD**. Slide cooking tray into the center position of the cooking chamber. Once cooked, transfer to serving tray and garnish with chopped green onions before serving.

TIP You can use a store-bought or homemade chili sauce for these ribs.

PANKO PICKLE SPEARS
WITH CREAMY DILLY DIP
MAKES 4 TO 6 SERVINGS

Combine tartness with a crispy batter and a creamy sauce with a spicy kick. These pickle spears will become a game-night snack favorite, weekend app-to-go and unique addition to any appetizer party.

PREP TIME
15 minutes

COOK TIME
10 minutes

VORTEX PROGRAM
▶ Air Fry

CREAMY DILLY DIP

¼ cup (60 mL) mayonnaise or vegan mayonnaise

2 tbsp (30 mL) regular or vegan sour cream

1 tsp (5 mL) dried or fresh dill, finely chopped

Salt and freshly ground black pepper

PANKO PICKLES

4 large dill pickles, split lengthwise into 4 spears

½ cup (125 mL) all-purpose flour or gluten-free flour

½ cup (125 mL) milk

½ tsp (2 mL) baking powder

½ tsp (2 mL) paprika, regular or smoked

½ tsp (2 mL) freshly ground black pepper

Panko bread crumbs, regular or gluten free

Olive oil cooking spray

1 *Creamy Dilly Dip:* In a bowl, combine mayonnaise, sour cream and dill. Mix well and season to taste with salt and pepper. Mix well and set aside.

2 *Panko Pickles:* Cut pickles into spears and lay on a paper towel–lined baking sheet. Pat dry so excess liquid is absorbed.

3 In a bowl, combine flour, milk, baking powder and paprika; mix well. Place seasoned panko in a separate shallow bowl.

4 Dip pickle spear first in flour mixture, then in panko, ensuring it is completely coated on all sides. Lay pickle on cooking tray, ensuring there is space between pickles and they are not overlapping. Repeat with remaining pickles, using both trays. Lightly spray pickles with cooking spray on all sides.

5 Place the drip pan in the bottom of the cooking chamber. Using display panel, select **AIR FRY**, set **TEMPERATURE** to 400°F (200°C) and set **TIME** to 10 minutes. **PREHEAT** Vortex until display indicates **ADD FOOD**.

6 Slide cooking trays into middle and bottom positions and close door. When display indicates **TURN FOOD**, turn pickles over on each cooking tray and switch bottom tray to top position and middle tray to bottom position. Cook until pickles are hot and crust is golden. Serve with the Creamy Dilly Dip.

TIP There are lots of variations of pickles. Feel free to use anything from spicy habanero to garlic.

SPINACH PUFFS

MAKES 12 SERVINGS

Whenever I need a total crowd-pleaser appetizer for a party, I turn to puff pastry. Pre-rolled sheets of buttery, flaky dough are endlessly versatile, bake up beautifully golden every time and can be found in the freezer section of any grocery store. These are filled with a simple mixture of frozen spinach and feta cheese, just like a classic spanakopita.

PREP TIME
20 minutes

COOK TIME
20 minutes

VORTEX PROGRAM
▶ Bake

1 bag (500 g) frozen chopped spinach, thawed

½ cup (125 mL) crumbled feta cheese

4 chopped green onions, white and green parts

1 tbsp (15 mL) chopped fresh parsley

1 tbsp (15 mL) chopped fresh mint

3 cloves garlic, minced

½ tsp (2 mL) salt

¼ tsp (1 mL) freshly grated pepper

2 eggs

1 sheet frozen puff pastry (about ½ lb / 250 g), thawed in refrigerator

1 Place spinach in a fine mesh colander and squeeze out all the excess water until the spinach is as dry as you can make it. Transfer to a large bowl.

2 To spinach, add cheese, green onions, parsley, mint, garlic, salt and pepper. In a small bowl, lightly beat 1 egg; add to spinach mixture and stir well to combine.

3 Lightly beat the other egg; set aside.

4 Unroll puff pastry and cut into four strips about 4 inches wide (10 cm). Cut each strip into three squares, about 4 inches (10 cm) long. You should get 12 equal squares from each piece of puff pastry. Divide filling and spoon onto the center of each square (about 2 tbsp/30 mL per square). Brush egg around the outside edges of square then fold pastry over, corner to corner, to make a triangle. Repeat until all filling is used up. Using a fork, lightly press tines around outside edges of pastry to seal edges. Place four triangles spaced apart on the cooking tray so that the points face each other. Chill or freeze remaining pastries until ready to bake.

5 Place drip pan in the bottom of cooking chamber. Using the display panel, select BAKE, adjust TEMPERATURE to 350°F (180°C) and set TIME to 20 minutes. PREHEAT Vortex until display indicates ADD FOOD.

6 Slide one cooking tray into middle position and cook until display indicates TURN FOOD. Turn triangles over and return tray to middle position. Cook until golden. Let cool 5 minutes before transferring to a wire rack and cool completely.

TIPS I found that it is best to bake only one tray at a time, but if you want to bake two trays of puffs, place one tray in the bottom and one tray in the middle position. When display indicates TURN FOOD, turn triangles over and switch bottom tray to top position and middle tray to bottom position.

To cook from frozen, add 2 more minutes to cooking time.

MAIN DISHES
BEEF

ASIAN FLANK STEAK

MAKES 4 TO 6 SERVINGS

This is one of my favorite ways to flavor flank steak, a very lean cut of beef that benefits from marinating. You can easily cook this to a medium-rare without smoking up the entire house! Leftovers make great-tasting sandwiches.

PREP TIME
5 minutes

MARINATING TIME
8 hours or overnight

COOK TIME
12 to 15 minutes

VORTEX PROGRAMS
▶ Air Fry
▶ Broil

¼ cup (60 mL) hoisin sauce

3 tbsp (45 mL) soy sauce

2 tbsp (30 mL) freshly squeezed lime juice

1 tbsp (15 mL) vegetable oil

4 cloves garlic, minced

2 tsp (10 mL) chili paste (such as sambal oelek)

1½ lb (750 g) flank steak

1 In a shallow dish, whisk together hoisin sauce, soy sauce, lime juice, vegetable oil, garlic and chili paste; add steak, turning to coat both sides with marinade. Refrigerate covered at least 8 hours or overnight. Remove meat from refrigerator 30 minutes before cooking.

2 Place the drip pan in the bottom of the cooking chamber. Using the display panel, select **AIR FRY**, adjust **TEMPERATURE** to 400°F (200°C) and set **TIME** to 15 minutes. **PREHEAT** Vortex until display indicates **ADD FOOD**.

3 Set cooking tray in the middle position. When display indicates **TURN FOOD**, turn the flank steak over and slide tray back into middle position. Close door and continue until steak reaches your desired doneness (15 minutes for medium-rare). If you like your steak medium, add 5 more minutes to cooking time.

4 Once cooking time is finished, remove tray from cooking chamber. Select **BROIL** on display panel and set **TIME** for 8 minutes. When display indicates **ADD FOOD**, slide cooking tray with steak into the top position. When display indicates **TURN FOOD**, turn steak over onto the other side. Continue to cook until lightly browned and slightly crisped on the edges.

5 Transfer steak to a cutting board, cover loosely with foil and let stand 10 minutes. Thinly slice at right angles to the grain of the meat.

TIPS Sambal oelek is an Indonesian chili paste is made up of crushed raw red chilies, vinegar and salt. It is available in most grocery stores in the Asian foods section. One tablespoon is the equivalent of a chopped small jalapeño.

If you can't find it, you can substitute 1 tsp (5 mL) hot sauce or ¼ tsp (1 mL) red hot pepper flakes.

KOREAN STEAK TACOS
MAKES 6 SERVINGS

Try this three-ingredient Korean Steak Taco recipe for a change. It's fast and the pickled cucumbers are ready by the time the steak is done.

1 recipe Asian Flank Steak

2 tbsp (30 mL) gochujang sauce

Six 6-inch flour tortillas, warmed

Quick Pickled Cucumbers

Toasted sesame seeds (optional)

1 Spread gochujang sauce on bottom of warm tortilla. Top with slices of flank steak. Garnish with Quick Pickled Cucumbers and sesame seeds.

TIP This is a gluten-free option if you don't use flour tortillas.

QUICK PICKLED CUCUMBERS
MAKES 4 SERVINGS

These pickled cucumbers are the perfect crunchy, tangy topping for the flank steak.

¼ cup (60 mL) rice wine vinegar

1 tsp (5 mL) granulated sugar

½ tsp (2 mL) salt

Freshly ground black pepper

2 English cucumbers, thinly sliced

1 tbsp (15 mL) finely chopped chives

1 In a bowl, combine rice wine vinegar, sugar, salt and pepper; whisk to combine. Add cucumber slices and chives and toss to combine.

2 Cover and refrigerate for at least 30 minutes or overnight to allow flavors to meld. Taste and season with additional salt and pepper if needed.

CARNE ASADA

MAKES 4 SERVINGS

My friend Sandra is from Dominican Republic and introduced me to skirt steak — a delicious cut of beef — a few years ago. It's quite forgiving and can be cut into smaller segments that fit perfectly in the Vortex. Her rules for making this dish? Use lots of lime juice and sautéed onions. She always makes it on the grill, so we decided to test it in on the Air Fry function. I was super impressed with the results, especially since I didn't have to go outside on a cold, snowy night to use my barbecue grill.

PREP TIME

10 minutes

MARINATING TIME

2 hours

COOK TIME

10 minutes

VORTEX FUNCTION

▶ Air Fry

---

2 oranges, juiced

4 limes, juiced

2 lbs (1 kg) skirt steak, cut into four or five pieces to fit the cooking trays

Olive oil cooking spray

2 medium onions, sliced

1 tbsp (15 mL) olive oil

Salt and freshly ground black pepper

2 limes, cut in half

▶ SHALLOW PAN OR SEALABLE BAG

1 In a shallow pan or sealable bag, combine orange juice and lime juice. Add pieces of steak, cover and refrigerate for at least 2 hours or overnight, turning the meat once or twice in the juice.

2 When you are ready to cook, using the display panel, select **AIR FRY**, set **TEMPERATURE** to 325°F (160°C) and set **TIME** to 10 minutes. **PREHEAT** Vortex until display indicates **ADD FOOD**.

3 While the oven preheats, toss onion slices with olive oil and season with salt and pepper. Place on drip pan.

4 Slide pan into middle position. When display indicates **TURN FOOD**, mix onions. Cook until softened and tender. Remove from cooking chamber and transfer to a bowl. Keep warm. Rinse off drip pan and place in the bottom of the chamber.

5 Remove steaks from marinade, place on cooking tray and dry off with paper towel. Season well with salt and pepper.

6 Using the display panel, select **AIR FRY**, adjust **TEMPERATURE** to 400°F (200°F) and set **TIME** to 10 minutes. **PREHEAT** Vortex until display indicates **ADD FOOD**.

7 Slide cooking tray into middle position. When display indicates **TURN FOOD**, turn steaks over, lightly spray second side, rearranging pieces so that any covered bits are exposed, and continue cooking until browned and sizzling.

8 Using kitchen tongs, transfer to a cutting board. Squeeze lime juice all over. Let stand 5 minutes, then carve across the grain into ½-inch (1 cm) thick slices.

TIPS Carne asada is usually made with skirt steak, but flank steak is a good alternative.

GREEK BEEF POCKETS

MAKES 4 SERVINGS

Beef burger patties are endlessly versatile. I've added lots of oregano plus some extra special seasonings for a Greek-inspired pita pocket.

PREP TIME
15 minutes

COOK TIME
9 minutes

VORTEX PROGRAM
▶ Air Fry
▶ Reheat

---

1 lb (500 g) lean ground beef

¼ cup (60 mL) fresh bread crumbs

2 cloves garlic, minced

2 tsp (10 mL) dried oregano

1 tsp (5 mL) paprika

½ tsp (2 mL) ground cinnamon

½ tsp (2 mL) freshly ground black pepper

¼ tsp (1 mL) ground allspice

4 feta cheese cubes, ½-inch by 1-inch (1 by 2.5 cm)

Salt

Olive oil cooking spray

Four 8-inch (20 cm) rounds pita bread

Baba ghanouj or tzatziki

Crumbled feta cheese

Baby spinach leaves

1 In a large bowl, mix together ground beef, bread crumbs, garlic, oregano, paprika, cinnamon, pepper and allspice. Blend just until combined. Measure out eight equal portions of meat mixture. Roll each portion into a ball then flatten into a patty. Place one cube of feta cheese into the top of one beef patty then place another beef patty on top and pinch edges to seal in the cheese. Lay patties on cooking tray. Sprinkle beef patties with salt on the outside, then spray with cooking spray.

2 Place drip pan in the bottom of cooking chamber. Using the display panel, select **AIR FRY**, adjust **TEMPERATURE** to 380°F (193°C) and set **TIME** to 9 minutes. **PREHEAT** Vortex until display indicates **ADD FOOD**.

3 Place cooking tray in middle position. When display indicates **TURN FOOD**, flip patties over. Cook until lightly browned, juices run clear when pierced and internal temperature reads 160°F (71°C) on meat thermometer.

4 While patties are resting, place pitas on cooking tray. Select **REHEAT**, set **TEMPERATURE** to 350 and set **TIME** to 5 minutes. Reheat until pitas are warm.

5 To assemble, spread baba ghanouj on pita. Add burger patty and top with baby spinach and crumbled feta cheese.

TIP Don't let leftover bread go to waste. Use up the ends and any stray pieces to make great bread crumbs. Simply break up pieces and place in a food processor, then grind until bread crumbs are formed.

FRIDAY NIGHT FAJITAS

MAKES 4 SERVINGS

I love this recipe because it's a quick and easy main dish, yet it calls for so few ingredients. Using the rotisserie basket allows everything to cook evenly and the meat is tender and juicy, while the peppers and onions still have a little crunch. While the meat and vegetables are cooking, set out bowls of grated cheese, sour cream and salsa and go to town.

PREP TIME
15 minutes

COOK TIME
10 minutes

VORTEX PROGRAMS
▶ **Air Fry**
▶ **Rotate**
▶ **Reheat**

FAJITA SEASONING

1 tbsp (15 mL) chili powder

1½ tsp (7 mL) ground cumin

1 tsp (5 mL) freshly ground black pepper

½ tsp (2 mL) smoked paprika, sweet or hot

½ tsp (2 mL) dried oregano

¼ tsp (1 mL) garlic powder

¼ tsp (1 mL) onion powder

¼ tsp (1 mL) red hot pepper flakes

continued →

▶ ROTISSERIE BASKET AND LIFT

1 *Fajita Seasoning:* In a bowl, combine chili powder, cumin, black pepper, smoked paprika, oregano, garlic and onion powder and hot pepper flakes; mix well.

2 *Friday Night Fajitas:* In a large bowl, mix together steak strips, onion and bell peppers; spray or add oil and sprinkle with Fajita Seasoning mix. Transfer mixture to rotisserie basket; securing lid in place.

3 Place the drip pan in the bottom of the cooking chamber. Using the rotisserie lift tool, lift the basket into the cooking chamber and slide the basket along the side bars until spit reaches the rotisserie hole. Pull forward on the red release lever to secure the ends of the basket in place. Close door.

4 Using the display panel, select **AIR FRY** and **ROTATE**, adjust **TEMPERATURE** to 400°F (200°C) and set **TIME** to 10 minutes. Press **START** and ignore display when it says **ADD FOOD**.

5 Once cooked, remove basket using rotisserie lift. Transfer to a large bowl and, using oven mitts, remove lid.

6 To serve, spoon meat and vegetable mixture down the center of tortilla; add garnishes of choice, leaving a little space at the top and more space on each side of the tortilla. Fold in sides, almost enough so they touch. Using your thumbs, bring the bottom flap over the sides. Continue pulling the bottom flap taut and use it to wrap over the filling, folding one or two more times, until the filling is encased in the tortilla.

FRIDAY NIGHT FAJITAS

1 lb (500 g) boneless sirloin or strip steak, cut into ¼-inch (0.5 cm) strips

1 medium onion, sliced

1 green or red bell pepper, cut into 2-inch (5 cm) strips

Oil spray or 1 tbsp (15 mL) olive oil

Eight 10-inch (25 cm) flour or gluten-free tortillas, warmed

GARNISHES

Sour cream, grated cheese, salsa, shredded lettuce, chopped fresh cilantro

TIPS To warm tortillas, wrap in foil. Place in Vortex on **REHEAT** and set **TEMPERATURE** to 350°F (180°C). Heat for 8 to 10 minutes. Or place four tortillas on a microwave-safe plate, cover it with a damp paper towel and microwave in 20-second bursts until they are warmed through.

For a gluten-free meal, choose gluten-free tortillas.

"I LOVE THIS RECIPE BECAUSE IT'S A QUICK AND EASY MAIN DISH, YET IT CALLS FOR SO FEW INGREDIENTS."

GARLIC-STUDDED ROTISSERIE ROAST BEEF

SERVES 4 TO 6

Slivers of garlic infuse this beef with a rich, garlicky flavor. And because you put it onto the rotisserie, it self-bastes, creating a beautifully caramelized and browned exterior and an exceptionally tender interior.

PREP TIME
10 minutes

COOK TIME
12 to 15 minutes/lb (500 g)

VORTEX PROGRAMS
▶ **Roast**
▶ **Rotate**

---

1 boneless top sirloin beef roast, 4 to 4½ lbs (2 to 2.5 kg) with a fat cap, trussed

2 large cloves garlic, sliced

1 tsp (5 mL) salt

½ tsp (2 mL) freshly ground black pepper

½ tsp (2 mL) garlic powder

▶ ROTISSERIE SPIT, FORKS AND LIFT

1 Remove the roast from the refrigerator and let stand at room temperature for 1 hour. Pat dry with paper towels. Do not remove butcher's string from roast.

2 With the point of a sharp knife, cut deep slits all over roast, including in the fat cap. Insert garlic slivers into slits, pushing them right down so they are under the surface of the beef.

3 Insert rotisserie spit through the center of the roast. Thread the rotisserie forks from each side of the roast, securing one fork into either side of the roast. Tighten the screws to secure the spit in place.

4 Season roast all over with a generous sprinkling of salt, pepper and garlic powder.

5 Place drip pan in the bottom of the cooking chamber. Using the rotisserie lift tool, lift the spit into the cooking chamber and slide the spit along the sidebars until the spit reaches the rotisserie hole. Pull forward on the red release lever to secure the ends of the spit in place. Close door.

6 Using the display panel, select **ROAST** and **ROTATE**, adjust **TEMPERATURE** to 380°F (193°C) and set **TIME** to the minutes per pound (or kilogram) based on the size of roast you have, about 60 minutes. Press **START**. Ignore display when it says **ADD FOOD**.

7 Cook beef until thermometer reads 140°F (60°C) for medium-rare, 160°F (71°C) for medium, about 45 to 60 minutes. (When taking the temperature, make sure thermometer does not touch the rotisserie spit.)

8 Remove from cooking chamber to a carving board. Cover loosely with foil and let stand 15 to 30 minutes before removing the spit and forks and carving. Carve into thin slices to serve.

TIPS Beef rotisserie roasts are simply boneless roasts cut from traditional oven roasts. They are tied so that they rotate easily on the rotisserie and cook up evenly. My favorite cuts for this recipe are eye of round, top sirloin, sirloin tip or outside round. Make sure you have a fat cap on the outside, as it will render its fat as is cooks, basting the meat all over, helping to keep it juicy and tender

A meat thermometer is essential to knowing which stage of doneness the roast has reached. Plunge the thermometer into the thickest part of the meat, but make sure it doesn't touch the metal parts of the rotisserie, as that will give you an inaccurate reading.

INSIDE-OUT CHEESEBURGER MINI MEATLOAVES

MAKES 12, FOR 4 TO 6 SERVINGS

These mini meatloaves are more like muffins, but make a great dinner and packable lunch. My chef friend Kate Dowhan created these fun muffins for her kids, but everyone enjoys them, no matter what age. All your favorite toppings are already included, even a special place for the ketchup.

PREP TIME
5 minutes

COOK TIME
13 minutes

VORTEX PROGRAM
▶ Air Fry

---

1 lb (500 g) lean ground beef

1 egg, lightly beaten

1 cup (500 mL) shredded Cheddar cheese, divided

1 small onion, finely chopped

¼ cup (60 mL) dry bread crumbs

2 tbsp (30 mL) green relish

2 tbsp (30 mL) mustard

2 tbsp (30 mL) ketchup

▶ 12 SILICONE MUFFIN CUPS

1 In a bowl, combine ground beef, egg, ½ cup (125 mL) cheese, onion, bread crumbs, relish and mustard. Mix thoroughly to blend.

2 Place ¼ cup (60 mL) of meat mixture into 12 silicone muffin cups. Make an indent in the center of each meat cup. Fill indents with ketchup. Sprinkle remaining cheese evenly over each meat cup.

3 Place six cups on each cooking tray, laying them around the outside edges of the tray, leaving the center of the tray empty.

4 Place the drip pan in the bottom of the cooking chamber. Using the display panel, select **AIR FRY**, then set **TEMPERATURE** to 375°F (190°C) and **TIME** to 13 minutes. **PREHEAT** Vortex until display indicates **ADD FOOD**.

5 Set cooking trays in the top and bottom positions of the cooking chamber. When display indicates **TURN FOOD**, switch trays so bottom tray moves to the top and top tray moves to the bottom.

6 Meatloaves are cooked when juices run clean and thermometer registers 160°F (71°C) when placed in the center of meatloaf.

TIPS I like to double this recipe and wrap extra cooked meatloaves in plastic wrap and foil to store in the freezer. To reheat, defrost overnight in the fridge, then microwave on medium until heated through.

VARIATIONS You can substitute ground turkey or chicken for the ground beef.

For a gluten-free option, substitute gluten-free bread crumbs or oats as a binder. Make sure your mustard is also gluten-free.

PERFECT STEAKS FOR TWO
WITH BLUE CHEESE CRUST

MAKES 2 SERVINGS

Although strip steaks are a smaller cut in the family of steaks, they are the perfect size for the Vortex. They also have a nice fat cap on the outside so they can form a light crust while staying rare or medium-rare on the inside.

PREP TIME
5 minutes

COOK TIME
12 to 15 minutes

VORTEX PROGRAMS
▶ Air Fry
▶ Broil

2 strip loin steaks, at least ½-inch (1 cm) thick

Salt and freshly ground black pepper

Nonstick cooking spray

¼ cup (60 mL) blue cheese, crumbled

¼ cup (60 mL) sour cream

1 Season all sides of strip steaks liberally with salt and pepper. Place steaks on one cooking tray. Spritz cooking spray over one side of steak.

2 Place drip pan in the bottom of the cooking chamber. Using the display panel, select AIR FRY, adjust TEMPERATURE to 375°F (190°C) and set TIME to 12 minutes for rare steak or 15 minutes for medium-rare. Press START. PREHEAT Vortex until display indicates ADD FOOD.

3 Slide cooking tray into middle position. When display indicates TURN FOOD, turn steaks over and spritz other side of steak with cooking spray.

4 Cook until steak is cooked and internal temperature indicates 130°F (55°C) for rare or 145°F (63°C) for medium-rare when measured with a meat thermometer.

5 In a bowl, combine cheese and sour cream. Divide mixture evenly over top of steaks.

6 Using the display panel, select BROIL, adjust TEMPERATURE to 400°F (200°C) and set TIME to 2 minutes. Press START. PREHEAT Vortex until display indicates ADD FOOD.

7 Slide cooking tray into top position. Cook until is cheese is slightly melted and bubbling.

TIPS In the Vortex, you want good air circulation around each steak, so Air Fry them in the middle position only.

THE DINER BURGER

MAKES 4 TO 6 SERVINGS

According to my chef friend Patrick, the best burgers contain three types of ground meat and only a good seasoning of salt and pepper. Having made many burgers, I totally agree with him. Keep it simple. There is no need for any other fillers, like bread crumbs or egg. The mixture of meats will keep these burgers tender and juicy.

PREP TIME
5 minutes

COOK TIME
9 minutes

VORTEX PROGRAMS
▶ Air Fry
▶ Broil

THE DINER BURGER

1 lb (500 g) extra lean ground beef

½ lb (250 g) medium ground beef

½ lb (250 g) ground pork

Salt and freshly ground black pepper

Nonstick cooking spray

6 cheese slices

MAYONNAISE SAUCE

⅓ cup (75 mL) mayonnaise

2 tbsp (30 mL) ketchup

2 tsp (10 mL) relish or chopped pickles

6 hamburger buns

TOPPINGS

Lettuce, tomato, sliced onions, cooked bacon

1 *The Diner Burger:* In a bowl, combine all the meats, gently mixing so you don't overmix. Shape and press into six patties, about ¼-inch (6 mm) thick. Press a divot into the center of each patty with your thumb. Season outsides of patties well with salt and pepper. Place three patties on each cooking tray, divot side down. Lightly spray both sides with cooking spray.

2 Place drip pan in the bottom of cooking chamber. Using the display panel, select **AIR FRY**, adjust **TEMPERATURE** to 375°F (190°C) and set **TIME** to 9 minutes. **PREHEAT** Vortex until display indicates **ADD FOOD**.

3 Place cooking trays in bottom and middle positions. When display indicates **TURN FOOD**, flip patties over so they are divot side up and switch bottom cooking tray to top position and middle cooking tray to bottom position. Cook until lightly browned, juices run clear when pierced and internal temperature reads 160°F (71°C) on meat thermometer.

4 Place cheese slice on top of each burger. Using the display panel, select **BROIL**, adjust **TEMPERATURE** to 400°F (200°C) and set **TIME** to 2 minutes. **PREHEAT** Vortex until display indicates **ADD FOOD**.

5 Place cooking tray one at a time in top position and cook until cheese is melted.

6 *Mayonnaise Sauce:* Meanwhile, in a small bowl, combine mayonnaise, ketchup and relish; mix well.

7 To assemble, spread Mayonnaise Sauce over inside of buns, place burger on bottom and garnish with toppings of your choice.

TIPS When cooking only one or two burgers, place cooking tray in middle position and, when Vortex indicates **TURN FOOD**, move tray to top position.

To prepare burgers from frozen, place frozen burgers on cooking tray. **PREHEAT** Vortex as above but set **TIME** to 12 minutes. Continue cooking as directed.

MAIN DISHES
LAMB

GYROS SKEWERS

MAKES 4 SERVINGS

Gyros are a tasty Mediterranean takeout treat made with ground lamb and spices. This time, since regular kabob sticks are too long for the Vortex, I have wrapped the seasoned meat around a cinnamon stick, adding another flavor to the meat sticks. Serve with tzatziki sauce and a Greek salad for the complete gyros experience.

PREP TIME
10 minutes

COOK TIME
12 minutes

VORTEX PROGRAM
▶ Air Fry

---

1 tsp (5 mL) ground rosemary

½ tsp (2 mL) ground coriander

½ tsp (2 mL) ground cumin

½ tsp (2 mL) ground cinnamon

1 tsp (5 mL) salt

½ tsp (2 mL) freshly ground black pepper

1 small onion, grated

1 clove garlic, grated

1 lb (500 mL) ground lamb

8 cinnamon sticks

Olive oil cooking spray

1 In the bottom of a large bowl, combine ground rosemary, coriander, cumin, cinnamon and salt and pepper; mix well. Add grated onion, garlic and ground lamb. Gently mix the meat and spices until the meat is evenly blended with the spices.

2 Divide the mixture into 2-oz (60 g) portions, each about the size of a golf ball. Wrap each portion around a cinnamon stick, using about three-quarters of the length of the stick, covering one end but leaving a little "handle" of cinnamon stick protruding from the other end. Place four covered sticks on each cooking tray, leaving a little space around each meat stick. Lightly spray with cooking spray.

3 Place drip pan in the bottom of the cooking chamber. Using the display panel, select **AIR FRY**, adjust **TEMPERATURE** to 375°F (190°C) and set **TIME** to 12 minutes. Press **START**. **PREHEAT** Vortex until display indicates **ADD FOOD**.

4 If you don't want to make all at once, use only one cooking tray, sliding tray into middle position. When display indicates **TURN FOOD**, turn meat sticks over. If using two trays, slide into middle and bottom positions. When display indicates **TURN FOOD**, turn meat sticks over and switch bottom tray to top position and middle tray to bottom position.

5 Cook until lightly browned, internal cooked temperature indicates 160°F (71°C) when measured with a meat thermometer and meat is no longer pink inside. Let sticks rest for 5 minutes before serving.

TIPS When mixing ground meat and spices together, clean, dry hands work better than mixing with a fork or spatula.

When forming the meat mixture around the cinnamon sticks, make sure you press the mixture enough so that it adheres to the stick and holds together.

Grind fresh or dried rosemary in a food processor or using a mortar and pestle until finely ground.

PEPPERED LAMB CHOPS

MAKES 2 TO 4 SERVINGS

I have two fantastic small local butcher shops where I like to buy my lamb. I adore lamb, but not everyone does. Once you try these chops, you'll realize how easy and tasty lamb can be.

PREP TIME
10 minutes

MARINATING TIME
Up to 30 minutes or up to 12 hours

COOK TIME
12 to 14 minutes

VORTEX PROGRAM
▶ Broil

---

4 lamb chops, about 12 oz (375 kg) total

2 tbsp (30 mL) soy sauce

1 tbsp (15 mL) olive oil

1 tbsp (15 mL) red wine vinegar

2 tsp (10 mL) coarsely crushed black peppercorns

1 tsp (5 mL) Dijon mustard

$\frac{1}{2}$ tsp (2 mL) garlic powder

$\frac{1}{2}$ tsp (2 mL) salt

1 Trim all but $\frac{1}{4}$-inch (5 mm) thickness of fat from chops; slash fat at $\frac{1}{2}$-inch (1 cm) intervals.

2 In a shallow dish, combine soy sauce, oil, vinegar, peppercorns, mustard, garlic powder and salt; add chops, turning to coat all over. Cover and marinate up to 30 minutes at room temperature or refrigerate for up to 12 hours. (If refrigerating, bring back to room temperature before cooking.)

3 Place lamb chops on cooking tray, reserving any marinade. Place drip pan in the bottom of the cooking chamber. Using the display panel, select **BROIL**, adjust **TEMPERATURE** to 400°F (200°C) and set **TIME** to 12 minutes for medium-rare or 14 minutes for medium. Press **START**. **PREHEAT** Vortex until display indicates **ADD FOOD**.

4 Slide cooking tray into middle positions. When display indicates **TURN FOOD**, turn chops over and brush other side with reserved marinade.

5 Cook chops until internal cooked temperature indicates 145°F (63°C) for medium-rare or 160°F (71°C) for medium when measured with a meat thermometer. Let chops rest for 5 minutes before serving.

TIP Slashing the fat on the outside edge of the chops helps to render the fat, making the fat crispy and tasty and the chops extra juicy and moist.

LAMB CHOPS
WITH MAPLE MUSTARD GLAZE

MAKES 2 SERVINGS

Lamb chops are wonderful "au naturel" but even more wonderful with a mustard glaze and sweet hint of maple. This is a quick way to dress them up when entertaining.

PREP TIME
5 minutes

MARINATING TIME
30 minutes up to 8 hours

COOK TIME
12 minutes

VORTEX PROGRAM
▶ **Broil**

MAPLE MUSTARD GLAZE

1 tbsp (15 mL) Dijon mustard

1 tbsp (15 mL) maple syrup

1 tbsp (15 mL) balsamic vinegar

1½ tsp (7 mL) finely chopped fresh rosemary (or ½ tsp/2 mL dried)

1 clove garlic, minced

½ tsp (2 mL) freshly ground black pepper

LAMB CHOPS

4 lamb loin chops, 1-inch (2.5 cm) thick, trimmed (about 1½ lbs/750 g)

Salt

1 *Maple Mustard Glaze:* In a shallow glass dish, combine mustard, maple syrup, balsamic vinegar, rosemary, garlic and pepper.

2 *Lamb Chops:* Add chops to Maple Mustard Glaze and turn them to coat. Marinate at room temperature for 30 minutes or longer and refrigerate, turning occasionally for up to 8 hours. (If refrigerated, bring back to room temperature before cooking.)

3 Place lamb chops on each cooking tray, reserving any marinade. Place drip pan in the bottom of the cooking chamber. Using the display panel, select **BROIL**, adjust **TEMPERATURE** to 400°F (200°C) and set **TIME** to 12 minutes for medium-rare or 14 minutes for medium. Press **START. PREHEAT** Vortex until display indicates **ADD FOOD**.

4 Slide one cooking tray into middle position. When display indicates **TURN FOOD**, turn chops over and brush other side with reserved marinade.

5 Cook chops until internal cooked temperature indicates 145°F (63°C) for medium-rare or 160°F (71°C) when measured with a meat thermometer. Let rest 5 minutes before serving. Season with salt to taste.

TIP The two most popular and tender cuts of lamb available in the supermarket are lamb loin and rib chops. Loin chops look like mini T-bone steaks, while rib chops are sometimes frenched, meaning the fat and meat along the bones have been cleaned off.

MUSTARD ROSEMARY ROTISSERIE LAMB ROAST

MAKES 4 TO 6 SERVINGS

This simple boneless leg of lamb takes on a rich, earthy flavor when studded with slivers of garlic and sprigs of rosemary and coated in Dijon mustard. Cooking lamb over the rotisserie evenly roasts and self-bastes the meat to absolute tender and juicy perfection.

PREP TIME
10 minutes

COOK TIME
12 to 15 minutes/lb (500 g) for medium-rare or 15 to 18 minutes/lb (500 g) for medium

VORTEX PROGRAMS
▶ **Roast**
▶ **Rotate**

---

1 boneless lamb leg roast, 4 to 4½ lbs (2 to 2.5 kg) with fat cap, tied

2 large cloves garlic, sliced

2 sprigs fresh rosemary, cut into 2-inch (5 cm) lengths

1 tsp (5 mL) salt

½ tsp (2 mL) freshly ground black pepper

2 tbsp (30 mL) Dijon mustard

▶ ROTISSERIE SPIT, FORKS AND LIFT

1 Remove the roast from the refrigerator and let stand at room temperature for 1 hour. Pat dry with paper towels. Do not remove butcher's string from roast.

2 With the point of a sharp knife, cut deep slits all over roast, including the fat cap; insert garlic slivers into slits, pushing them right down so they are under the surface of the lamb. Tuck rosemary sprigs into any folds of meat and under the butcher's string.

3 Insert rotisserie spit through the center of the roast. Thread rotisserie forks from each side of the roast, securing one fork into either side of the roast. Tighten screws to secure the spit in place.

4 Season roast all over with a good sprinkling of salt and pepper, and brush Dijon mustard all over lamb.

5 Place drip pan in the bottom of the cooking chamber. Using the rotisserie lift tool, lift the spit into the cooking chamber and slide the spit along the sidebars until the spit reaches the rotisserie hole. Pull forward on the red release lever to secure the ends of the spit in place. Close door.

6 Using the display panel, select **ROAST** and **ROTATE**, adjust **TEMPERATURE** to 380°F (193°C) and set **TIME** to the minutes per pound (or kilogram) based on the size of roast you have, between about 45 to 60 minutes. Press **START**.

7 Cook lamb until thermometer reads 145°F (63°C) for medium-rare, 160°F (71°C) for medium, about 45 to 60 minutes. (Make sure when taking the temperature that the thermometer does not touch the metal parts of the rotisserie.)

8 Remove from cooking chamber to a carving board. Cover loosely with foil and let stand 15 to 30 minutes before removing the spit and forks or carving. Carve into thin slices to serve.

TIPS Leftovers topped with a dollop of tzatziki, slices of sweet onion, tomatoes, cucumber and crumbled feta make delicious sandwiches.

Always use a meat thermometer. That is your best indicator of which stage of doneness a roast has reached. Plunge thermometer into the thickest part of the meat, but make sure it doesn't touch the metal parts of the rotisserie, as that will give you an inaccurate reading.

"COOKING LAMB OVER THE ROTISSERIE EVENLY ROASTS AND SELF-BASTES THE MEAT TO ABSOLUTE TENDER AND JUICY PERFECTION."

MAIN DISHES
PORK

ALL-DRESSED BACON-WRAPPED FRANKFURTERS

MAKES 4 SERVINGS

This recipe is just plain fun wrapped up in a bun. You can be as creative as you wish with the toppings, but this combination has a Mexican twist that makes it a party in a pan!

PREP TIME

10 minutes

COOK TIME

Air Fry: 10 minutes

Broil: 3 minutes

VORTEX PROGRAMS

▶ **Air Fry**

▶ **Broil**

1 large onion, sliced

1 tbsp (15 mL) olive oil

Salt and freshly ground black pepper

4 jumbo frankfurters

8 slices bacon

4 top-cut hot dog buns

1 cup (250 mL) shredded smoked Gouda cheese

½ cup (125 mL) guacamole

Pickled jalapeño peppers

1 Toss onion slices with olive oil and season with salt and pepper. Place on drip pan.

2 Using the display panel, select **AIR FRY**, set TEMPERATURE to 325°F (160°C) and set TIME to 10 minutes. **PREHEAT** Vortex until display indicates **ADD FOOD**.

3 Slide tray into middle position. When display indicates **TURN FOOD**, stir onions. Cook until softened and tender.

4 Meanwhile, wrap each frankfurter with two slices of bacon and place on cooking tray. Using the display panel, select **AIR FRY**, adjust TEMPERATURE to 400°F (200°C) and set TIME to 10 minutes. **PREHEAT** Vortex until display indicates **ADD FOOD**.

5 Slide cooking tray into middle position. When display indicates **TURN FOOD**, turn frankfurters over. Continue to cook until bacon is cooked. For crispier bacon, cook 2 minutes longer.

6 Open hot dog buns and sprinkle with cheese. Place on cooking tray. Set display to **BROIL**, set time for 2 minutes. Place in middle position and broil until cheese is melted.

7 To assemble, place frankfurter in hot dog bun, top with guacamole, pickled jalapeños and cooked onions.

TIP Look for hot dog buns that are cut from the top rather than side-cut buns. It is easier to load up on the toppings and the bun is less likely to split.

JAMAICAN JERK ROTISSERIE PORK

MAKES 4 SERVINGS

Need a little spice in your life? This marinade packs lots of flavor and some heat too, but don't be alarmed, as it's gently toned down once it cooks on the rotisserie. In Jamaica, this is street food eaten with rice and peas, grilled corn or a fried cornbread.

PREP TIME
15 minutes

MARINATING TIME
8 hours or overnight

COOK TIME
40 to 50 minutes

VORTEX PROGRAMS
▶ **Roast**
▶ **Rotate**

2 tbsp (30 mL) soy sauce

1 tbsp (15 mL) prepared dry jerk marinade

2 scotch bonnet peppers, seeded

6 cloves garlic, minced

2 tbsp (30 mL) brown sugar

1 tbsp (15 mL) freshly minced gingerroot

1 boneless pork loin roast, 3½ to 4 lbs (1.75 to 2 kg), preferably rib or tenderloin end

▶ ROTISSERIE SPIT, FORKS AND LIFT
▶ SHALLOW PAN OR SEALABLE BAG

1 In a blender combine soy sauce, jerk marinade, peppers, garlic, brown sugar and ginger; blend until smooth.

2 Cut small slits into pork roast all over, to allow marinade to seep into the meat. Place meat in a shallow roasting pan or sealable bag and pour marinade over. Allow meat to marinate overnight, making sure it is completely covered with marinade.

3 Remove meat from marinade. Insert the spit into pork roast through the center. Thread rotisserie forks from each side, securing one fork into either end. Tighten screws to secure spit in place.

4 Place the drip pan in the bottom of the cooking chamber. Using the rotisserie lift tool, lift the spit into the cooking chamber and slide the spit along the sidebars until spit reaches the rotisserie hole. Pull forward on the red release lever to secure the ends of the spit in place. Close door.

5 Using the display panel, select **ROAST** and **ROTATE**, adjust **TEMPERATURE** to 350°F (180°C) and set **TIME** for 50 minutes. Press **START**.

6 Pork is cooked when juices run clear and thermometer inserted in center registers 160°F (71°C). Remove roast from cooking chamber and transfer to a cutting board. Tent with foil and let stand for 10 minutes before removing spit and forks.

TIP Pressed for time? You can use a ready-made store-bought liquid marinade and skip making this one from scratch.

CHINESE-STYLE PORK TENDERLOIN

MAKES 2 TO 4 SERVINGS

Pork tenderloin is one of the most versatile cuts of pork. I like to serve this with steamed Thai jasmine rice and a green vegetable such as bok choy or asparagus.

PREP TIME
10 minutes

MARINATING TIME
1 hour or overnight

COOK TIME
18 minutes

VORTEX PROGRAMS
▶ **Roast**
▶ **Rotate**

Two 1 lb (500 g) pork tenderloins, trimmed of any fat and silver skin

3 tbsp (45 mL) soy sauce

1 tbsp (15 mL) hoisin sauce

1 tsp (5 mL) sesame oil

2 cloves garlic, grated

1 tsp (5 mL) grated gingerroot

▶ ROTISSERIE BASKET AND LIFT
▶ SHALLOW BOWL OR SEALABLE BAG

1 In a shallow bowl or sealable storage bag, mix together soy sauce, hoisin sauce, sesame oil, garlic and ginger. Add pork tenderloins and marinate 1 hour, or up to 24 hours refrigerated.

2 Remove tenderloins from marinade and place in rotisserie basket. Secure lid on basket. Place drip pan in the bottom of cooking chamber. Using the rotisserie lift tool, lift the rotisserie basket into the cooking chamber and slide along the side bars until spit reaches the rotisserie hole. Pull forward on the red release lever to secure the ends of the spit in place. Close door.

3 Using the display panel, select **ROAST** and **ROTATE**, adjust **TEMPERATURE** to 380°F (180°C) and set **TIME** to 18 minutes. Press **START**.

4 Cook until browned and internal temperature reads 145°F (63°C) when tested with a thermometer.

TIPS There is often a light gray layer of connective tissue on pork tenderloin. This is known as the silver skin. It needs to be removed before you cook the tenderloin. Slide a sharp knife under the silver skin and peel it away from the meat and discard it.

I like to grate the garlic and ginger in this recipe so I don't lose as much in the cooking process while it is in the rotisserie basket.

To avoid gluten, substitute a gluten-free alternative for soy sauce, such as tamari or hoisin sauce.

BANH MI PORK & RICE BOWLS

MAKES 4 SERVINGS

If you've ever had a Vietnamese Banh Mi sandwich, you probably know the bread can sometimes overpower the pork and other wonderful flavors. So this time I've put it all into a bowl, using the pork recipe from Chinese-Style Pork Tenderloin (page 74). It's fresh, bright and oh-so-tasty!

PREP TIME
10 minutes

1 recipe Chinese-Style Pork Tenderloin (page 74)

PICKLED CARROTS

6 tbsp (90 mL) white vinegar

1/4 cup (60 mL) granulated sugar

1/4 tsp (1 mL) salt

1 cup (250 mL) shredded carrots

ASIAN DRESSING

2 tbsp (30 mL) soy sauce

1 tbsp (15 mL) sesame oil

2 tbsp (30 mL) rice wine vinegar

2 tbsp (30 mL) olive oil

1/2 tsp (2 mL) grated gingerroot

BOWLS

3 cups (750 mL) cooked brown rice, quinoa, barley or grain of your choice

2 cups (250 mL) prepared Asian coleslaw mixture

1/2 English cucumber, thinly sliced

1 small jalapeño pepper, minced

1/4 cup (60 mL) fresh cilantro

1 *Chinese-Style Pork Tenderloin:* Remove pork from marinade, and transfer marinade to a small saucepan. Bring marinade to a boil over high heat and simmer 2 minutes (or heat in microwave on High for 1 minute).

2 Cook pork tenderloin according to directions for Chinese-Style Pork Tenderloin on page 74. Allow meat to cool, slice into thin slices, and then cut slices crosswise so you have strips. Place in a bowl, pour warm sauce over pork and let sit.

3 *Pickled Carrots:* In a bowl, combine vinegar, sugar and salt; stir until sugar is dissolved. Add carrots and let sit for about 30 minutes. Drain well and refrigerate until ready to use.

4 *Asian Dressing:* In a large jar, combine soy sauce, sesame oil, rice wine vinegar, olive oil and ginger. Shake well to blend. Store in refrigerator until ready to use.

5 *Bowls:* Place about 3/4 cup (175 mL) rice in each bowl. Top each with 1/3 cup (75 mL) pork, 1/4 (60 mL) cup Asian coleslaw mixture, 1/4 cup (60 mL) cucumber slices, 1/4 cup (60 mL) pickled carrots, jalapeño and fresh cilantro. Drizzle with Asian dressing.

TIPS I often use the coarse grate on my box grater to make the carrots. However, you can use just your knife to create matchstick slices of carrots. Cut carrot slices on a diagonal then cut slices into matchstick pieces. The thinner they are, the more they will soften up and pickle in the vinegar.

To cook brown rice, use the long-grain variety. Rinse it first to wash away any grit and dust from the production process. In a large saucepan, combine 1 cup (250 mL) rice, 2 cups (500 mL) water and 1 tsp (5 mL) salt. Bring to a boil, reduce heat to low, then cover and simmer on low for 45 minutes. Make sure there is no more that about 1 tbsp (15 mL) of water left in the pot. Remove from heat and let rice rest for about 10 minutes, then fluff and serve.

HONEY DIJON PORK SCHNITZEL

MAKES 4 SERVINGS

This version of schnitzel is crazy delicious. The term *schnitzel* refers to the cooking method of pounding meat to tenderize it and then bread and fry it. The air fryer function creates a delicious browned crust with just a light spray of cooking oil.

PREP TIME
20 minutes

COOK TIME
12 minutes

VORTEX PROGRAMS
▷ Air Fry

2 tbsp (30 mL) freshly squeezed lemon juice

1 tbsp (15 mL) liquid honey

1 tbsp (15 mL) Dijon mustard

2/3 cup (150 mL) dry seasoned bread crumbs

1/4 cup (60 mL) grated Parmesan cheese

1/2 tsp (2 mL) salt

1/4 tsp (1 mL) freshly ground black pepper

1 lb (500 g) boneless pork chops, pounded thin

Sauerkraut, warmed

Nonstick cooking spray

1 In a bowl, combine lemon juice, honey and mustard. In a shallow bowl, combine bread crumbs, cheese, salt and black pepper. Dip pork into lemon juice mixture, then into breadcrumbs, and lay on two cooking trays. Spray pork schnitzels on both sides with cooking spray.

2 Place drip pan in the bottom of the cooking chamber. Using the display panel, select **AIR FRY**, adjust **TEMPERATURE** to 375°F (190°C) and set **TIME** to 12 minutes. Press **START**. **PREHEAT** Vortex until display indicates **ADD FOOD**.

3 If using one tray, slide cooking tray into middle position. When display indicates **TURN FOOD**, turn schnitzel over. If using two trays, slide them into middle and bottom positions. When display indicates **TURN FOOD**, turn schnitzels over and switch bottom tray to top position and middle tray to bottom position.

4 Cook until lightly browned, internal cooked temperature indicates 160°F (71°C) when measured with a meat thermometer and meat is no longer pink inside. Let rest for 5 minutes before serving. Serve with warm sauerkraut.

TIPS It's important to lightly spray the schnitzel with oil before cooking to ensure you get a nice golden color.

I used boneless center-cut pork chops, but you can also use slices of pork tenderloin. Pound to about 1/4-inch (0.5 cm) thick. Don't pound them too thin, or they will dry out in cooking.

For a gluten-free alternative, substitute ground pork rinds in place of the panko or use gluten-free panko bread crumbs instead.

CAESAR PORK BURGERS

MAKES 4 SERVINGS

Everyone will love the flavor of their favorite salad in these juicy burgers. They are especially tasty if you serve a Caesar salad alongside the burger.

PREP TIME
10 minutes

COOK TIME
12 minutes

VORTEX PROGRAMS
▶ Air Fry
▶ Broil

---

1 egg

1 lb (500 g) lean ground pork

¼ cup (60 mL) freshly grated Parmesan cheese, divided

¼ cup (60 mL) panko bread crumbs

2 strips bacon, finely chopped

1 clove garlic, minced

1 tbsp (15 mL) lemon juice

2 tsp (10 mL) anchovy paste

1 tbsp (15 mL) Worcestershire sauce

Salt

¼ tsp (1 mL) freshly ground black pepper

Olive oil cooking spray

4 Kaiser buns

4 leaves romaine lettuce

1 In a medium bowl, beat egg. Add pork, 2 tbsp (30 mL) cheese, panko, bacon, garlic, lemon juice, anchovy paste and Worcestershire sauce. Mix well and shape into four patties, about ¾-inch (2 cm) thick. Using your thumb, press a divot into the middle of one side of the burger. Season burger on both sides with salt and pepper. Place burgers on cooking tray, divot side down. Lightly spray with cooking spray.

2 Place drip pan in the bottom of cooking chamber. Using the display panel, select **AIR FRY**, adjust **TEMPERATURE** to 380°F (180°C) and set **TIME** to 12 minutes. **PREHEAT** Vortex until display indicates **ADD FOOD**.

3 When display indicates **TURN FOOD**, flip patties over so they are divot side up. Continue to cook until lightly browned, juices run clear when pierced and internal temperature reads 160°F (71°C) on meat thermometer.

4 Place remaining Parmesan on top of each burger. Using the display panel, select **BROIL**, adjust **TEMPERATURE** to 400°F (200°C) and set **TIME** to 2 minutes. **PREHEAT** Vortex until display indicates **ADD FOOD**.

5 Place cooking tray in top position and cook until cheese is melted.

6 To serve, place burgers on buns; top with romaine lettuce.

TIPS If desired, combine 1 tbsp (15 mL) olive oil with 1 clove of grated garlic. Brush over cut side of Kaiser buns and place on cooking tray in top position. Set Vortex to Broil and broil for 2 minutes.

It's important to take the internal temperature of ground meats to ensure they are fully cooked. Insert a meat thermometer into the side of the burger so it reaches the center.

SAUSAGE & PEPPER HERO

MAKES 4 SERVINGS

This fun combination is one to write home about. It's especially worth it if your pasta sauce is homemade, but store-bought also works. Call it a hero with or without melted mozzarella, but naturally I love it with the gooey melted cheese.

PREP TIME

15 minutes

COOK TIME

20 minutes

VORTEX PROGRAMS

▶ **Air Fry**

▶ **Rotate**

▶ **Broil**

---

1 yellow or orange bell pepper, sliced

1 medium onion, sliced

1 tbsp (15 mL) olive oil

1 tsp (5 mL) dried basil

½ tsp (2 mL) salt

¼ tsp (1 mL) freshly ground black pepper

4 mild or hot Italian sausages

4 crispy Italian hero rolls, 6 to 8 inches (15 to 20 cm) long

1 cup (250 mL) prepared pasta sauce

4 slices mozzarella cheese

▶ ROTISSERIE BASKET AND LIFT

1 In a large bowl, mix together bell peppers, onions, olive oil and basil. Toss to combine so vegetables are well coated with the oil. Transfer mixture to rotisserie basket, adding sausages into basket as well. Secure lid in place.

2 Using the rotisserie lift tool, lift the basket into the cooking chamber and slide the basket along the side bars until spit reaches the rotisserie hole. Pull forward on the red release lever to secure the ends of the basket in place. Close door.

3 Place the drip pan in the bottom of the cooking chamber. Using the display panel, select **AIR FRY** and **ROTATE**, adjust **TEMPERATURE** to 360°F (182°C), and set **TIME** to 20 minutes. Cook sausage mixture until sausages are browned, juices run clear when pierced and internal temperature registers 160°F (71°C) when tested with a thermometer. Once cooked, remove rotisserie basket using lift tool. Using oven mitts, remove lid and transfer mixture to a large bowl; keep warm.

4 Open the rolls and place on two cooking trays. Add a layer of pasta sauce on bottom half of rolls. Then place sausage, top with peppers and onions, and cover with a slice of mozzarella.

5 Using the display panel, select **BROIL**, adjust **TEMPERATURE** to 400°F (200°C) and set **TIME** to 2 minutes. Press **START** to preheat.

6 When display indicates **ADD FOOD**, slide tray into middle position. Cook until the cheese has started to melt and the bread is beginning to get toasty. Remove and serve at once.

TIPS Be sure to keep your eye on the heros once they are under the broiler. Don't let them burn. If you are cooking four sandwiches, do it in two batches so you can use the middle position.

Look for a roll that is slightly crisp on the outside and soft on the inside.

GARLIC BUTTER PORK CHOPS

MAKES 4 SERVINGS

GF

These chops are juicy, tender and super-flavorful thanks to the amazing garlic-butter thyme sauce. It's fast and easy to prep — in 5 minutes you'll have everything Vortex ready!

PREP TIME
5 minutes

COOK TIME
8 minutes

VORTEX PROGRAM
▶ Air Fry

4 boneless pork loin chops,
½ inch (1 cm) thick
(about 1 lb/500 g)

Kosher salt

Freshly ground
black pepper

2 tbsp (30 mL) softened
butter

1 large garlic clove, finely
minced

½ tsp (2 mL) dried thyme

1 Season pork chops all over with salt and pepper; set aside.

2 In a small bowl, mix together softened butter, garlic and thyme. Place half of the butter mixture on top of each pork chop. Lay two pork chops on each cooking tray.

3 Place the drip pan in the bottom of the cooking chamber. Using the display panel, select **AIR FRY**, adjust **TEMPERATURE** to 400°F (200°C) and set **TIME** for 8 minutes, then press **START**. **PREHEAT** Vortex until display indicates **ADD FOOD**.

4 Set cooking trays on middle and bottom position. When the display indicates **TURN FOOD**, turn the chops over, adding remaining garlic butter onto each chop. Switch the cooking trays so that the tray that was in the center position is now in the bottom position, and the one that was at the bottom is now at the top.

5 Close door and continue to cook until internal cooked temperature reaches 155°F (68°C). Remove chops and let rest for 3 to 5 minutes.

TIPS Choose dried thyme in the leaf form rather than ground, as it has more flavor and the oils don't release as quickly. You can also substitute oregano or herbes de Provence, a fragrant dry seasoning blend from the south of France that owes some of its unique flavor culinary lavender.

STICKY FIVE-SPICE RIBS

MAKES 2 SERVINGS

Laden with a tangy, garlicky glaze that's spiked with fragrant Chinese five-spice powder, these ribs are impressive. There's no grilling, just a simple slow roasting in the Vortex with a quick broil at the end for a delicious tender rack of ribs. Cut them into smaller portions for an appetizer if you wish, but in my house, it's the whole rack or nothing!

PREP TIME
15 minutes

MARINATING TIME
4 hours or up to 24 hours

COOK TIME
1 hour + 2 minutes

VORTEX PROGRAMS
▷ **Roast**
▷ **Broil**

---

1 rack (2 lbs/1 kg) baby back ribs, cut in half

2 tbsp (30 mL) rice wine vinegar

1 tbsp (15 mL) brown sugar

1 tbsp (15 mL) oyster sauce

1 tsp (5 mL) Chinese five-spice powder

2 cloves garlic, minced

▶ SEALABLE BAG

1 Place ribs in sealable bag. In a glass measure, combine vinegar, brown sugar, oyster sauce, Chinese five-spice powder and garlic; mix together and pour over ribs, making sure they are well coated. Marinate in refrigerator for 4 hours or up to 24 hours.

2 Transfer ribs to cooking tray, reserving marinade.

3 Place drip pan in the bottom of the cooking chamber. Pour water into the bottom of the drip pan.

4 Using the display panel, select **ROAST**, adjust **TEMPERATURE** to 300°F (150°C) and set **TIME** for 60 minutes. Press **START** and preheat Vortex until display indicates **ADD FOOD**.

5 Slide cooking tray into middle position. Cook ribs until meat is pulling back from bones and they are tender. Remove from cooking chamber and let rest for 5 minutes

6 Meanwhile, place reserved marinade in small saucepan. Bring to boil, reduce heat and simmer 3 minutes until thickened.

7 Brush ribs generously on both sides with cooked marinade. Place back on cooking tray. Using display panel, select **BROIL**, adjust **TEMPERATURE** to 400°F (200°C) and set **TIME** to 2 minutes. When display indicates **ADD FOOD**, slide tray into middle position. **BROIL** until ribs are glazed and bubbling.

TIPS Chinese five-spice powder is a fragrant blend of five key seasonings — cinnamon, cloves, fennel, star anise and Szechuan peppercorns. Sometimes it might also contain ground ginger and nutmeg. Most major grocery stores carry this seasoning in their spice aisle or, if they have a good international aisle, you can find it there too.

MAIN DISHES
POULTRY

BARBECUED TAKEOUT-STYLE ROTISSERIE CHICKEN

MAKES 4 SERVINGS

Who doesn't like to pick up a ready-barbecued takeout chicken from the grocery store? They make quick meals and are great for salads and sandwiches the next day. Using the rotisserie function on the Vortex, you can easily make your own in less than an hour. Make sure you rub the seasoning mixture under the wings and legs too, to get the chicken completely coated with flavor.

PREP TIME
10 minutes

COOK TIME
40 minutes

VORTEX PROGRAMS

▶ **Roast**

▶ **Rotate**

ROTISSERIE CHICKEN

1 chicken (about 3½ lbs/1.75 kg), trussed

Olive oil

BARBECUED TAKEOUT-STYLE RUB

1 tbsp (15 mL) onion powder

2 tsp (10 mL) paprika

1 tsp (5 mL) garlic powder

1 tsp (5 mL) dried oregano flakes

1 tsp (5 mL) dried thyme flakes

1 tsp (5 mL) brown sugar

1 tsp (5 mL) salt

½ tsp (2 mL) dried rosemary

½ tsp (2 mL) dried ground sage

1 *Rotisserie Chicken:* Insert rotisserie spit into the chicken through the neck, coming out through the bottom cavity. Thread the rotisserie forks from each side, securing one fork into either side of the chicken breast and the other into the chicken thighs. Tighten the screws to secure the spit in place.

2 If using a spray bottle, spray oil all over chicken, including under back, wings and legs. Or gently rub a little oil over all sides of chicken with your hands.

3 *Barbecued Takeout-Style Rub:* In a bowl, combine onion powder, paprika, garlic powder, oregano, thyme, brown sugar, salt, rosemary and sage, mixing well. Sprinkle or rub 2 tbsp (30 mL) of seasoning mix over all sides of chicken, including under the wings and creases between the legs. Set aside.

4 Place the drip pan in the bottom of the cooking chamber. Using the rotisserie lift tool, lift spit into the oven and slide spit along the side bars until spit reaches the rotisserie holes. Pull forward on the red release lever to secure the ends of the spit in place. Close the door.

5 Using the display panel, select **ROAST** and **ROTATE**, then adjust **TEMPERATURE** to 380°F (180°C) and set **TIME** for 45 minutes. Press **START**. Chicken is cooked when juices run clear when chicken is pierced and thermometer inserted in thigh registers 185°F (85°C).

6 Remove chicken from the oven and let stand 10 to 15 minutes before loosening forks and removing spit from inside the chicken.

TIP Make sure you purchase a roasting chicken no larger than 4 lbs (2 kg); otherwise, it will be too heavy for the rotisserie. I like them already trussed — that way I just spray and rub. What could be easier?

CHILI BUTTER RUBBED CHICKEN BREASTS

MAKES 4 SERVINGS

GF

A little sweet with a little spice — sometimes the simplicity is all we need. Butter rubbed under and over the skin produces a nice crisp skin and super juicy meat.

PREP TIME
10 minutes

COOK TIME
35 minutes

VORTEX PROGRAM
▶ Roast

¼ cup (60 mL) unsalted butter

1 tbsp (15 mL) chili powder

½ tsp (2 mL) salt

¼ tsp (1 mL) hot pepper flakes

2 cloves garlic, minced

4 bone-in, skin-on chicken breasts

1 In a small bowl, combine butter, chili powder, salt, hot pepper flakes and garlic; mix well.

2 Gently poke your fingers under the skin of each chicken breast and lift the skin slightly. Being careful not to tear the membrane that connects the skin to the chicken, gently push some of the chili butter between layers, massaging to even out. Then rub a little on the top of chicken breast. Repeat with the other three chicken breasts.

3 Lay chicken breast side down on two cooking trays.

4 Place drip pan in the bottom of the cooking chamber. Using the display panel, select ROAST, then adjust TEMPERATURE to 380°F (180°C). Set TIME to 30 minutes. Press START. PREHEAT Vortex until display indicates ADD FOOD.

5 Slide cooking trays into top and bottom-most positions. When display indicates TURN FOOD, flip chicken breasts over so they are breast side up, then switch bottom cooking tray to top position and top tray to bottom position. Brush chicken with melted butter from the drip pan.

6 Cook until chicken is golden brown, juices run clear when pierced and chicken is no longer pink inside and internal cooked temperature indicates 165°F (74°C) when measured with a meat thermometer.

TIP The advantage to using bone-in chicken breasts for this recipe is that the bone helps keep the chicken moist and tender as it distributes the heat more evenly through the meat. The skin also seals in the moisture and juiciness.

CHICKEN CORDON BRIE

MAKES 4 SERVINGS

We all know those delicious frozen chicken bundles stuffed with ham or broccoli and cheese. This version takes chicken to a new level by stuffing it with Brie cheese and mango, then rolling in corn flakes crumbs for a crispy coating. They are a perfect choice for entertaining.

PREP TIME
15 minutes

COOK TIME
12 minutes

VORTEX PROGRAM
▶ Air Fry

---

4 skinless, boneless chicken breasts

Salt and freshly ground black pepper

1 mango, peeled and sliced into long thin wedges

4 oz (125 g) Brie or Camembert cheese

½ cup (125 mL) corn flakes or other crispy cereal crumbs

½ tsp (2 mL) dried thyme

Olive oil cooking spray

¼ cup (60 mL) balsamic glaze

▶ KITCHEN STRING OR 4 BAMBOO SKEWERS

1 Place chicken breasts between two pieces of plastic wrap and pound to an even thickness of about ⅛-inch (3 mm) thickness. Season chicken with salt and pepper. Arrange mango slices down the center of each breast. Cut cheese lengthwise into four pieces and place a piece on each breast. Roll up breast to enclose the filling. Secure with kitchen string or bamboo skewers. Season outside of chicken with salt and pepper.

2 In a shallow dish, combine corn flakes crumbs, thyme and ½ tsp (2 mL) salt and ¼ tsp (1 mL) pepper. Roll chicken in crumbs mixture to coat all over, and place two rolls on each cooking tray. (If only cooking two, see Step 4 and the Tip, below.) Spray both sides of rolls with cooking spray.

3 Place drip pan in the bottom of the cooking chamber. Using the display panel, select **AIR FRY**, adjust **TEMPERATURE** to 350°F (180°C) and set **TIME** to 15 minutes. Press **START**. **PREHEAT** Vortex until display indicates **ADD FOOD**.

4 If using one tray, slide cooking tray into middle position. When display indicates **TURN FOOD**, turn chicken breasts over. If using two trays, slide into top and bottom positions. When display indicates **TURN FOOD**, turn rolls over and switch bottom tray to top position and top tray to bottom position.

5 Cook until lightly browned, internal cooked temperature indicates 160°F (71°C) when measured with a meat thermometer and meat is no longer pink inside. Let rolls rest for 5 minutes before serving. Drizzle with balsamic glaze.

TIP Rolls can be completely prepared to the end of Step 2, but do not spray with cooking spray. Refrigerate up to 4 hours. Bring to room temperature for 30 minutes before cooking. **PREHEAT** Vortex as indicated above. Spray chicken just before putting in cooking chamber.

CHICKEN SALTIMBOCCA

MAKES 4 SERVINGS

GF

The Italian word saltimbocca means "jump in the mouth," and you will understand what that means when you make this recipe. Traditionally it's made with veal, but this version is irresistible. With so few ingredients, it's a perfect weeknight meal, but don't be afraid to serve it to company too.

PREP TIME
10 minutes

COOK TIME
10 minutes

VORTEX PROGRAM
▶ Air Fry

4 skinless, boneless chicken breasts

Freshly ground black pepper

8 fresh sage leaves

Shaved Parmesan or asiago cheese

4 to 8 large thin slices prosciutto

Olive oil cooking spray

¼ cup (60 mL) Marsala or port wine

¼ cup (60 mL) chicken stock

1 tbsp (15 mL) chopped fresh sage leaves

1 Place chicken breasts between two pieces of plastic wrap and pound them to an even thickness of ¼-inch (0.5 cm). Sprinkle each chicken breast with pepper.

2 Lay two sage leaves on top side of chicken, and then place shavings of cheese over top of sage leaves. Gently wrap one or two slices of prosciutto around chicken, tucking ends under the bottom of the breasts. Place two breasts on each cooking tray. Lightly spray tops of chicken with cooking spray.

3 Place drip pan in the bottom of the cooking chamber. Using the display panel, select **AIR FRY**, adjust **TEMPERATURE** to 400°F (200°C) and set **TIME** to 10 minutes. Press **START. PREHEAT** Vortex until display indicates **ADD FOOD**.

4 If using one tray, slide cooking tray into middle position. When display indicates **TURN FOOD**, turn chicken pieces over. If using two trays, slide into middle and bottom positions. When display indicates **TURN FOOD**, turn pieces over and switch bottom tray to top position and middle tray to bottom position.

5 Cook until lightly browned, internal cooked temperature indicates 160°F (71°C) when measured with a meat thermometer and meat is no longer pink inside. Let chicken rest for 5 minutes before serving.

6 Meanwhile, in a saucepan, combine Marsala and chicken stock; bring to a boil, reduce to a simmer and continue to cook for 5 to 7 minutes until reduced and slightly thickened. Stir in chopped sage; simmer 1 minute.

7 To serve, place chicken on serving plate and drizzle with Marsala sauce.

TIPS Recipe can be made in advance to the end of Step 2, but don't spray with cooking spray. Refrigerate, covered up to 6 hours in advance. Let chicken come to room temperature for 30 minutes before cooking. Spray with cooking oil spray just before placing in cooking chamber.

Two places in Italy are famed for their prosciutto — the province of Parma near Bologna, and the northeastern region of Friuli. The celebrated salted and air-cured ham is made elsewhere, inside and outside Italy, but the prosciutto di Parma and Friuli's prosciutto de San Daniele are widely recognized as the country's finest.

"WITH SO FEW INGREDIENTS, IT'S A PERFECT WEEKNIGHT MEAL, BUT DON'T BE AFRAID TO SERVE IT TO COMPANY TOO."

CHINESE TAKEOUT SESAME CHICKEN WITH BROCCOLI

MAKES 4 SERVINGS

Who needs takeout when you have this tasty chicken dish? It's sweet, salty, sticky and a little bit spicy — it covers all the bases. Letting the coated chicken breast nuggets sit for a few minutes before adding them to the rotisserie basket ensures you get a light crispy coating.

PREP TIME
15 minutes

COOK TIME
10 minutes

VORTEX PROGRAMS
▶ **Air Fry**
▶ **Rotate**

SAUCE

3 tbsp (45 mL) soy sauce or tamari

3 tbsp (45 mL) ketchup

3 tbsp (45 mL) honey

2 tbsp (30 mL) chili paste (such as sambal oelek)

2 tbsp (30 mL) brown sugar

1 tbsp (15 mL) sesame oil

1 tbsp (15 mL) rice wine or white wine vinegar

2 cloves garlic, finely chopped

1 tbsp (15 mL) finely chopped gingerroot

continued →

▶ ROTISSERIE BASKET AND LIFT

1 *Sauce:* In a bowl, combine soy sauce, ketchup, honey, chili paste, brown sugar, sesame oil, vinegar, garlic and ginger; mix well and set aside.

2 *Chinese Takeout Sesame Chicken with Broccoli:* Place cornstarch in one shallow bowl and beaten eggs in another; set aside. In a third bowl, combine flour, salt, pepper, paprika and garlic powder; mix well.

3 Dredge chicken first in cornstarch, then dip in eggs, making sure all sides of the chicken are covered in egg wash, and then dredge in flour mixture. Set pieces on cooking trays. Lightly spray chicken pieces with cooking spray. Let stand for 10 minutes, then place chicken in the rotisserie basket.

4 Place the drip pan in the bottom of the cooking chamber. Using the rotisserie lift tool, lift the basket into the cooking chamber and slide along the sidebars until the basket reaches the rotisserie hole. Pull forward on the red release lever to secure the ends of the basket in place. Close door.

5 Using the display panel, select **AIR FRY** and **ROTATE**, then set **TEMPERATURE** to 400°F (200°C) and set **TIME** to 10 minutes. Cook until chicken is lightly golden. When cooking is complete, remove rotisserie basket from the cooking chamber using the lift tool and allow basket to cool slightly before opening.

CHINESE TAKEOUT SESAME CHICKEN WITH BROCCOLI

2 eggs, lightly beaten

3 tbsp (45 mL) cornstarch

½ cup (125 mL) all-purpose flour, or gluten-free flour

1 tsp (5 mL) salt

½ tsp (2 mL) freshly ground black pepper

½ tsp (2 mL) paprika

½ tsp (2 mL) garlic powder

1 lb (500 g) boneless, skinless chicken breasts, cut in 1-inch (2.5 cm) pieces

Nonstick cooking spray

1 tbsp (15 mL) vegetable oil

1 onion, sliced

1 head broccoli, cut into florets

Steamed rice

Sesame seeds

6 In a skillet or wok, heat oil over high heat. Add onion and broccoli florets and stir-fry 2 minutes until tender crisp. Add Sauce ingredients and chicken; bring to a boil and cook 2 minutes until sauce is glossy and has slightly thickened. Serve immediately over rice. Garnish with sesame seeds.

TIP You don't need a rice cooker to make perfectly steamed rice. Rinse rice thoroughly in a colander until the water runs clear. I use a ratio of 2 cups (500 mL) water to 1 cup (250 mL) uncooked rice plus ½ tsp (2 mL) salt. This results in 3 cups (750 mL) of cooked rice. Bring water to a boil, add the salt, stir then add the rinsed and drained rice. Reduce the heat, cover the pot and simmer for 18 to 20 minutes. Remove it from the heat and let stand 5 minutes, then remove lid and fluff with a fork.

CRISP PARMESAN CHICKEN CAPRESE

MAKES 4 SERVINGS

GF

Two Italian classics — chicken Parmesan and fresh mozzarella caprese — combine in one. Parmesan-coated chicken, topped with more cheese and cherry tomatoes, makes a lighter version of the traditional fried dish that is sure to be everyone's new favorite meal.

PREP TIME
15 minutes

COOK TIME
8 minutes + 4 minutes

VORTEX PROGRAMS
▶ Air Fry
▶ Broil

2 skinless, boneless chicken breasts or 4 chicken scaloppini

Salt and pepper

¼ cup (60 mL) all-purpose flour

1 egg, lightly beaten

½ to 1 cup (125 to 250 mL) freshly grated Parmesan cheese (amount depends on how finely grated your cheese is)

¾ tsp (3 mL) dried oregano, divided

½ tsp (2 mL) dried basil

Oil spray

4 slices mozzarella cheese

½ cup (125 mL) halved cherry tomatoes

¼ cup (60 mL) prepared pesto

1 Cut chicken breasts horizontally through the center to create two thin cutlets. Place chicken between two pieces of plastic wrap and pound to an even thickness, about ¼ inch (0.5 cm). Pat dry and season with salt and pepper.

2 Place flour in a shallow bowl. In another shallow bowl, beat eggs with 1 tbsp (15 mL) water. In a third shallow bowl, mix Parmesan cheese with ½ tsp (2 mL) oregano and basil.

3 Dredge each piece of chicken with flour, then dip into egg, making sure to coat each piece well. Then dip each piece into Parmesan cheese mixture, pressing cheese onto both sides of chicken. Place chicken on two cooking trays, ensuring there is space around each piece of chicken. Lightly spray each piece of chicken with oil spray.

4 Place drip pan in the bottom of the cooking chamber. Using the display panel, select **AIR FRY**, adjust **TEMPERATURE** to 400°F (200°C) and set **TIME** to 8 minutes. Press **START**. **PREHEAT** Vortex until display indicates **ADD FOOD**.

5 Slide cooking trays into middle and bottom positions. When display indicates **TURN FOOD**, flip chicken pieces over and switch bottom cooking tray to top position and middle cooking tray to bottom position.

6 Cook until chicken is lightly golden, juices run clear when pierced and chicken is no longer pink inside and internal cooked temperature indicates 165°F (74°C) when measured with a meat thermometer.

7 Place mozzarella cheese slices on top of each piece of chicken. Spread cherry tomatoes evenly over cheese, cut-side down. Sprinkle with additional ¼ tsp (1 mL) dried oregano.

8 Using the display panel, select **BROIL**, adjust **TEMPERATURE** to 400°F (200°C) and set **TIME** to 4 minutes. **PREHEAT** Vortex until display indicates **ADD FOOD**.

9 Slide cooking trays into top and bottom positions. When display indicates **TURN FOOD**, switch bottom cooking tray to top position and top cooking tray to bottom position. Cook until mozzarella cheese is melted and tomatoes are roasted.

10 To serve, spread pesto in the center of the plate, about 1 tbsp (15 mL) per serving. Place chicken on top of pesto.

TIP To make ahead, prepare the chicken up to the end of Step 3, but don't spray with cooking spray. Place pieces on a plate, cover and refrigerate up to 8 hours before cooking.

"THIS LIGHTER VERSION OF THE TRADITIONAL FRIED DISH IS SURE TO BE EVERYONE'S NEW FAVORITE MEAL."

QUICK FIX CHICKEN WINGS

MAKES 4 SERVINGS

This recipe has been a favorite of my family's for years. The Vortex makes perfectly crispy, juicy chicken wings and we just toss them in the sticky sauce afterward. They are deliciously messy, so be sure to have plenty of paper napkins on hand.

PREP TIME
5 minutes

COOK TIME
25 minutes

VORTEX PROGRAMS
▶ **Air Fry**
▶ **Rotate**

½ cup (125 mL) brown sugar

¼ cup (60 mL) regular or gluten-free soy sauce

2 tbsp (30 mL) cider vinegar

1 clove garlic, minced

1 chicken bouillon cube, crushed

¼ tsp (1 mL) freshly ground black pepper

2 lbs (1 kg) split chicken wings

▶ ROTISSERIE BASKET AND LIFT

▶ SEALABLE BAG

1 In a bowl, combine brown sugar, soy sauce, cider vinegar, garlic, bouillon cube and pepper; stir to combine. Transfer to a sealable bag and add chicken wings; allow chicken to sit in mixture for 4 hours or overnight.

2 Drain chicken wings, reserving marinade. Place chicken wings in rotisserie basket.

3 Place the drip pan in the bottom of the cooking chamber. Using the rotisserie lift tool, lift the basket into the cooking chamber and slide the basket along the side bars until basket reaches the rotisserie hole. Pull forward on the red release lever to secure the ends of the spit in place. Close door.

4 Using the display panel, select **AIR FRY** and **ROTATE**, adjust **TEMPERATURE** to 360°F (182°C) and set **TIME** to 25 minutes. Press **START**.

5 Meanwhile add reserved marinade to a pot. Bring mixture to a boil, reduce heat and simmer 3 to 5 minutes or until slightly thickened.

6 Once chicken wings have finished cooking, remove rotisserie basket using lift tool and allow to stand 5 minutes to cool. Unlock lid and transfer chicken wings to a bowl. Toss with warm sauce and serve.

TIPS Try to purchase split chicken wings for this recipe. It makes it much easier to prepare rather than having to split them yourself.

HOISIN-GLAZED CHICKEN SALAD
WITH CABBAGE SLAW

MAKES 4 SERVINGS

For a bold contrast to the sweet glaze that coats these chicken thighs, this salad is served with a vibrant cabbage and carrot slaw tossed with a creamy mix of mayonnaise and gochujang, a fermented chili bean paste.

PREP TIME
15 minutes

COOK TIME
12 minutes

VORTEX PROGRAM
▶ Air Fry

HOISIN-GLAZED CHICKEN

⅓ cup (75 mL) hoisin sauce

4 tsp (20 mL) rice wine vinegar

1 tbsp (15 mL) soy sauce

4 skinless, boneless chicken thighs, about 1½ lbs (375 g)

2 green onions, white and green part, chopped

1 can (8 oz/227 g) water chestnuts, finely chopped

1 tbsp (15 mL) finely chopped gingerroot

CABBAGE SLAW

¼ cup (60 mL) mayonnaise

2 tsp (10 mL) chili bean paste (such as gochujang)

1 tbsp (15 mL) rice wine vinegar

1 package (381 g) Asian slaw mix

1 carrot, grated

3 tbsp (45 mL) chopped roasted cashews

1 *Hoisin-Glazed Chicken:* In a bowl, combine hoisin sauce, vinegar and soy sauce; mix well. Divide mixture into two bowls and set one aside.

2 Brush chicken thighs on both sides with one portion of the hoisin mixture. Place chicken on one cooking tray.

3 Place drip pan in the bottom of the cooking chamber. Using the display panel, select **AIR FRY**, adjust **TEMPERATURE** to 380°F (180°C) and set **TIME** to 12 minutes. Press **START**. **PREHEAT** Vortex until display indicates **ADD FOOD**.

4 Slide cooking trays into middle positions. When display indicates **TURN FOOD**, flip chicken pieces over and continue to cook until thighs are browned and beginning to blacken on the outside edges. Juices should run clear when pierced and temperature should measure 165°F (74°C) in thickest part of thigh. Let chicken rest for 5 minutes, then transfer to a cutting board and chop.

5 Transfer chicken to a bowl. Add green onions, water chestnuts, ginger and remaining hoisin sauce mixture; mix well. Refrigerate until ready to serve.

6 *Cabbage Slaw:* Meanwhile in a bowl, combine mayonnaise, gochujang paste and vinegar; mix well. Add slaw and carrot and toss well to mix.

7 To serve, divide slaw mixture onto serving plate. Top with chicken salad. Garnish with chopped cashews.

TIP Gochujang paste can be tricky to find. You will find it in an Asian or specialty grocery store; however, you can replace it in this recipe with an Asian-style hot sauce such as Sriracha sauce.

PECAN CURRIED CHICKEN CUTLETS

MAKES 4 SERVINGS

These moist chicken breasts have a decadent crispy coating that makes them easy weeknight fare yet elegant enough for company too. Serve with a crisp salad and roast potatoes and everyone will be asking for a second cutlet!

PREP TIME
10 minutes

COOK TIME
12 minutes

VORTEX PROGRAMS
▶ Air Fry

---

4 skinless, boneless chicken breasts

1 cup (250 mL) pecan halves

½ cup (125 mL) corn flakes cereal crumbs

1 tsp (5 mL) curry powder

½ tsp (2 mL) salt

2 tbsp (30 mL) mayonnaise

Olive oil cooking spray

2 tbsp (30 mL) raspberry balsamic vinegar

2 tsp (10 mL) liquid honey

▶ FOOD PROCESSOR

1 Place chicken between two pieces of plastic wrap and pound to an even ¼-inch (0.5 cm) thickness.

2 Place pecans, corn flakes crumbs, curry powder and salt in a food processor and process until finely chopped. Spread mixture onto a shallow plate. Brush mayonnaise evenly over both sides of chicken. Dip each chicken breast in the pecan mixture to coat well. Lay two pieces on each cooking tray. Spray both sides of cutlet with cooking spray.

3 Place drip pan in the bottom of the cooking chamber. Using the display panel, select **AIR FRY**, adjust **TEMPERATURE** to 375°F (190°C) and set **TIME** to 12 minutes. Press **START. PREHEAT** Vortex until display indicates **ADD FOOD**.

4 If using one tray, slide cooking tray into middle position. When display indicates **TURN FOOD**, turn chicken cutlets over. If using two trays, slide into middle and bottom positions. When display indicates **TURN FOOD**, turn cutlets over and switch bottom tray to top position and middle tray to bottom position.

5 Cook until lightly browned, internal cooked temperature indicates 160°F (71°C) when measured with a meat thermometer and meat is no longer pink inside. Let cutlets rest for 5 minutes before serving.

6 In a bowl, combine balsamic vinegar and honey; blend until mixed together. Drizzle over chicken cutlets before serving.

TIPS Chicken can be coated, covered and refrigerated for up to 4 hours before cooking.

To make cutlets, place chicken pieces between sheets of plastic wrap or parchment paper. Pound with a meat mallet or other household tool such as the back of a large spoon, wooden rolling pin, wine bottle or even a heavy book.

THAI ROTISSERIE CHICKEN

MAKES 4 TO 6 SERVINGS

If you have been to Thailand, you know that barbecued chicken is a classic street food. Every vendor has their own guarded recipe for kai yang. You can recreate this time-honored dish using the rotisserie feature in the Vortex instead of going out to the barbecue.

PREP TIME
20 minutes

COOK TIME
45 minutes

VORTEX PROGRAMS
▶ **Roast**
▶ **Rotate**

3 tbsp (45 mL) yellow curry paste

2 tbsp (30 mL) brown sugar

2 tbsp (30 mL) soy sauce

1 tbsp (15 mL) finely chopped cilantro stems

1 tbsp (15 mL) fish sauce

1 tbsp (15 mL) dry sherry (optional)

5 cloves garlic, minced

2 tsp (10 mL) freshly ground white pepper

1 roasting chicken (3 to 3½ lbs /1.5 to 1.75 kg), trussed

▶ ROTISSERIE SPIT, FORKS AND LIFT
▶ BLENDER OR FOOD PROCESSOR (OPTIONAL)
▶ LARGE SEALABLE BAG

1 In a blender or food processor, combine curry paste, brown sugar, soy sauce, cilantro, fish sauce, sherry (if using), garlic and pepper; blend until you have a paste. (Or you can mix this in a bowl. Just make sure you finely chop the garlic and cilantro.)

2 Loosen the skin around the chicken breast. Take a handful of marinade and rub it under the skin. Pour remaining marinade into a large sealable bag and place chicken in the bag. Massage marinade in and around the chicken; squeeze the air from the bag and seal. Marinate in the refrigerator for 4 hours or overnight.

3 Remove chicken from the marinade and pat dry outside surface. Truss chicken, ensuring wings are tucked under the back and legs are tied together.

4 Insert rotisserie spit through the cavity of the chicken. Thread the rotisserie forks from each side, securing one fork into either side of the chicken breast and the other into the chicken thighs. Tighten the screws to secure the spit in place.

5 Place drip pan in the bottom of the cooking chamber. Using the rotisserie lift tool, lift the spit into the cooking chamber and slide the spit along the side bars until the spit reaches the rotisserie hole. Pull forward on the red release lever to secure the ends of the spit in place. Close door.

6 Using the display panel, select **ROAST** and **ROTATE**, adjust **TEMPERATURE** to 380°F (193°C) and set **TIME** to 45 minutes. Press **START**. Chicken is cooked when juices run clear when chicken is pierced and thermometer inserted in thigh registers 185°F (85°C).

7 Once cooking chamber is cool, remove chicken using the lift tool and allow chicken to rest 10 to 15 minutes before loosening forks and removing spit from inside the chicken.

TIPS Make sure you purchase a roasting chicken no larger than 4 lbs (2 kg); otherwise, it will be too heavy for the rotisserie. If you have a larger chicken (maximum 5 lbs/2.5 kg), you will have to roast it on the roasting pan. Roasting temperature remains the same, but cooking time will increase to 1 hour.

Yellow curry paste is a blend of chilies, lemongrass, galangal (Asian ginger), Kaffir lime rind and leaves, fish sauce and spices including turmeric. It is milder compared to green or red curry paste, so if you prefer a little more heat, change up the type you use.

I like to serve this chicken with an easy pickled cucumber salad: Mix ⅓ cup (75 mL) with 1 tbsp (15 mL) granulated sugar and a pinch of salt, 1 Thai chili, finely chopped, 2 tbsp (30 mL) chopped fresh cilantro and 1 thinly sliced English cucumber. Mix in a bowl and garnish with chopped peanuts.

THE BEST BUTTERMILK-BRINED FRIED CHICKEN

MAKES 4 TO 6 SERVINGS

The first step toward really great fried chicken is a really great brine. Brining infuses the meat with savory finger-lickin' flavors, all while tenderizing it to butter-soft texture. Buttermilk also adds a delicious tanginess, making this chicken doubly good.

PREP TIME
15 minutes

MARINATING TIME
Overnight (minimum 8 hours)

COOK TIME
28 minutes

VORTEX PROGRAM
▶ Air Fry

BUTTERMILK BRINE

2 tbsp (30 mL) salt

1 tbsp (15 mL) granulated sugar

1 tsp (5 mL) celery seeds

1 tsp (5 mL) dried rosemary, crumbled

1 tsp (5 mL) freshly ground black pepper

1 bay leaf, crumbled

2 cups (500 mL) buttermilk

2 cloves garlic, grated

1 shallot, grated

2 lbs (1 kg) chicken drumsticks and thighs, skin on and bone in

continued →

▶ SEALABLE BAGS

▶ FINE MESH STRAINER

1 *Buttermilk Brine:* In a large sealable bag, place salt, sugar, celery seeds, rosemary, pepper and bay leaf. Pour in buttermilk, then add grated garlic and shallot. Seal the bag and shake to combine.

2 Add chicken and seal the bag, pushing out as much air possible, so the chicken is submerged in the buttermilk. Refrigerate overnight.

3 *Coating:* In a large freezer bag or bowl, combine flour, onion powder and paprika; set aside. Strain reserved brine through a fine mesh strainer and transfer into a bowl. Remove chicken from the buttermilk brine, reserving brine. Transfer chicken onto paper-towel lined tray and dry off chicken, removing any extra bits of spices. Place panko bread crumbs in a sealable bag or bowl.

4 Shake chicken first in seasoned flour mixture, then dip into reserved buttermilk, then into seasoned panko to coat evenly. Place chicken pieces evenly on cooking trays, taking care not to overcrowd the trays and ensuring there is as much air space around each piece as possible. (They should not overlap or even touch). Generously coat chicken pieces with oil spray on both sides.

5 Place the drip pan in the bottom of the cooking chamber. Using the display panel, select **AIR FRY**, adjust **TEMPERATURE** to 350°F (180°C) and set **TIME** to 28 minutes. **PREHEAT** Vortex until display indicates **ADD FOOD**.

COATING

1 cup (250 mL) all-purpose or gluten-free flour

1 tbsp (15 mL) onion powder

2 tsp (10 mL) paprika

2 cups (500 mL) seasoned panko bread crumbs, regular or gluten-free

Oil spray

Honey

6 Slide the two cooking trays into the top and bottom positions. When display indicates **TURN FOOD**, turn chicken pieces over and switch cooking trays so the tray that was in the bottom position is now in the top position and the top tray is now in the bottom position.

7 Close door and continue to cook until crust is golden brown and crisp and thermometer inserted into meat registers 165°F (74°C). Transfer to a serving plate, then drizzle with honey before serving.

TIPS If you want to double or triple these amounts for a crowd, you must air fry the pieces in batches because they must lie in a single layer on the cooking trays.

Panko is a Japanese-style bread crumb traditionally used to provide a light breaded coating to many deep-fried dishes. They allow the food to stay crispier longer than traditional bread crumbs. Because they are processed differently, they result in shard-like flakes rather than tiny grains.

"THE FIRST STEP TOWARD REALLY GREAT FRIED CHICKEN IS A REALLY GREAT BRINE."

TAMARIND & YOGURT MARINATED CHICKEN

MAKES 4 SERVINGS

Yogurt does incredible things to chicken. It soaks into the meat and makes the chicken more flavorful and tender and even a bit creamy. Serve this dish with cooked rice and roasted vegetables, or slice and tuck into a sandwich or wrap for a picnic the next day.

PREP TIME
10 minutes

MARINATING TIME
2 to 4 hours or overnight

COOKING TIME
14 minutes

VORTEX PROGRAM
▶ Air Fry

¼ cup (60 mL) whole milk plain yogurt

2 tbsp (30 mL) tamarind date sauce

2 tbsp (30 mL) freshly squeezed lemon juice

1 tbsp (15 mL) freshly squeezed lime juice

1 tsp (5 mL) freshly grated gingerroot

1 tbsp (15 mL) garam masala

1 tsp (5 mL) ground cumin

1 tsp (5 mL) turmeric

1 tsp (5 mL) salt

¼ tsp (1 mL) cayenne pepper (optional)

8 skinless, boneless chicken thighs

▶ BOWL OR SEALABLE BAG

1 In a bowl or sealable bag, combine yogurt, tamarind sauce, lemon and lime juice, ginger, garam masala, cumin, turmeric, salt and cayenne, if using. Add chicken to marinade and completely coat with yogurt mixture. Refrigerate for 2 to 4 hours or overnight.

2 Place the drip pan in the bottom of the cooking chamber. Using the display panel, select **AIR FRY**, adjust **TEMPERATURE** to 400°F (200°C) and set **TIME** to 15 minutes. Press **START**. **PREHEAT** Vortex until display indicates **ADD FOOD**.

3 Place chicken onto cooking trays, ensuring each piece has space around it so nothing is overlapping. Slide one cooking tray into the bottom position and the other tray into the top position. When indicator signals **TURN FOOD**, switch cooking trays so that the tray that was in the top position is now in the bottom position and the other tray moves to the top position. Continue to cook until chicken is slightly browned and internal temperature reads 165°F (74°C) and juices run clear when pierced.

TIPS Tamarind date sauce is a sauce made from the tamarind fruit. While tamarind paste is sold in many Indian grocery stores, this condiment sauce is usually mixed with dates and is more liquid. Look for it in aisles where you find prepared cooking and marinating sauces.

Garam masala is a blend of ground spices that are toasted and used extensively in Indian cooking. The word masala means "spices" while garam means "hot;" however, I never find it spicy. Find this blend in the spice or international aisle of the grocery store.

TUSCAN LEMON & HERB CHICKEN LEGS

MAKES 4 SERVINGS

We love roast chicken in the summertime, but who wants to heat up the kitchen with an oven? The Vortex makes the perfect cooking chamber. These legs are wonderfully crisp and juicy with bright lemon and herb flavor. If you wish, you can substitute three bone-in chicken breasts for the legs in this simple and easy recipe.

PREP TIME
10 minutes

MARINATING TIME
4 hours or overnight

COOK TIME
40 minutes

VORTEX PROGRAM
▶ **Roast**

---

4 whole chicken legs, trimmed of excess fat

2 lemons, zested and juiced

2 tbsp (30 mL) olive oil

1 tbsp (15 mL) finely chopped fresh oregano (or 1 tsp/5 mL dried)

1 tbsp (15 mL) finely chopped fresh rosemary (or 1 tsp/5 mL dried)

1 tsp (5 mL) salt, divided

½ tsp (2 mL) freshly ground black pepper

▶ **SHALLOW PAN OR SEALABLE BAG**

1 Place chicken legs in a shallow pan or sealable bag; set aside.

2 In a bowl, combine lemon zest and juice, olive oil, oregano, rosemary, ½ tsp (2 mL) salt and pepper; mix well and pour over chicken, ensuring it's completely coated. Cover and marinate in the refrigerator at least 4 hours or overnight.

3 Remove chicken from marinade, then lay pieces skin-side down on two cooking trays; discard marinade.

4 Place the drip pan in the bottom of the cooking chamber. Using the display panel, select **ROAST**, then set **TEMPERATURE** to 380°F (193°C) and set **TIME** to 40 minutes. **PREHEAT** Vortex until display indicates **ADD FOOD**.

5 Set cooking tray in the bottom and top positions. When display indicates **TURN FOOD**, turn the chicken legs over and switch cooking trays so that tray that was in the bottom position moves to the top position and top tray moves to bottom position. Close door and continue to cook until chicken legs are golden brown, juices of chicken run clear pierced and thermometer registers 185°F (85°C).

TIPS If cooking only one or two chicken legs, place cooking tray in middle position of cooking chamber. Cook as directed above.

The best way to zest citrus fruit is to use a Microplane®, box grater, vegetable peeler or paring knife to remove the outer layer of skin. Be sure not to dig too deep or overgrate. If using a vegetable peeler or paring knife, remove and discard the bitter white pith from inside the skin and finely chop zest.

ASIAN TURKEY MEATBALLS
WITH HOISIN LIME SAUCE

MAKES 18 TO 20 MEATBALLS, 4 SERVINGS

These Asian-inspired meatballs are out of this world. Made with ground turkey, ginger, green onions and sesame, they are delicious served over rice or cauliflower rice as an entrée, or pack them up with some Boston leaf lettuce for a carb-free lunch!

PREP TIME
20 minutes

COOK TIME
12 minutes

VORTEX PROGRAM
▶ Air Fry

ASIAN TURKEY MEATBALLS

1 lb (500 g) ground turkey

½ cup (125 mL) panko bread crumbs

2 tbsp (30 mL) soy sauce

2 tbsp (30 mL) hoisin sauce

1 tbsp (15 mL) brown sugar

3 cloves garlic, minced

1 tbsp (15 mL) finely chopped gingerroot

1 tbsp (15 mL) Asian chili sauce (such as sambal oelek)

2 green onions, white and green parts, finely chopped

¼ cup (60 mL) chopped fresh cilantro

continued →

1 *Asian Turkey Meatballs:* In a large bowl, use your hands to gently combine ground turkey, bread crumbs, soy sauce, hoisin sauce, garlic, ginger, Asian chili sauce, green onions and cilantro.

2 Shape mixture into 2-inch (5 cm) diameter meatballs and place on cooking trays around the edges, leaving the center of the cooking tray open.

3 Place drip pan in the bottom of the cooking chamber. Using the display panel, select **AIR FRY**, adjust **TEMPERATURE** to 375°F (190°C) and set **TIME** to 12 minutes. **PREHEAT** Vortex until display indicates **ADD FOOD**. Slide cooking trays into bottom and top positions.

4 When display indicates **TURN FOOD**, switch cooking trays so that tray in the top position moves to the bottom position and the tray in the bottom position moves to the top. Turn meatballs over to other side.

5 *Hoisin Lime Sauce:* In a small saucepan, combine hoisin sauce, water, sesame oil, lime juice and green onion. Cook over medium heat until heated through. Serve over meatballs.

6 Serve over rice topped with grated carrot and toasted sesame seeds. Drizzle Hoisin Lime Sauce over top.

HOISIN LIME SAUCE

3 tbsp (45 mL) hoisin sauce

3 tbsp (45 mL) water

1½ tsp (7 mL) sesame oil

1½ tsp (7 mL) lime juice

1 green onion, white and green parts, chopped

2 cups (500 mL) cooked white rice

1 small carrot, peeled and grated

Toasted sesame seeds

TIP Hoisin sauce is very popular in Southern Chinese cuisine. This dark, rich sauce is sweet and salty at the same time. Its base is made from soy beans and its distinctive taste comes from Chinese five-spice powder. Find it in the Asian food section of the grocery store.

INDIAN TURKEY BURGERS

MAKES 4 SERVINGS

Another burger alternative — but it's the toppings that make it special. The burgers can be formed, covered and refrigerated for up to 6 hours ahead.

PREP TIME
5 minutes

COOK TIME
8 minutes

VORTEX PROGRAM
▶ Air Fry

---

1 lb (500 g) ground turkey

2 cloves garlic, minced

1 egg, lightly beaten

1 tsp (5 mL) curry powder

1 tsp (5 mL) garam masala

1 cup (250 mL) fine dry bread crumbs, regular or gluten-free

1 tsp (5 mL) salt

½ tsp (2 mL) finely ground black pepper

Nonstick cooking spray

4 naan bread, about 6 inches (15 cm) round, warmed

Raita

Mango chutney

1 In a mixing bowl, combine ground turkey, garlic, egg, curry powder, garam masala, bread crumbs, salt and pepper; shape into four patties. (They will feel stickier than regular burgers). Make a thumb divot in the center of each patty. Place on two cooking trays, divot side down. Spray patties lightly with cooking spray.

2 Using the display panel, select **AIR FRY**, adjust **TEMPERATURE** to 375°F (190°C) and set **TIME** to 8 minutes. **PREHEAT** Vortex until display indicates **ADD FOOD**.

3 Place cooking trays in bottom and middle positions. When display indicates **TURN FOOD**, flip patties over so they are divot side up and switch bottom cooking tray to top position and middle cooking tray to bottom position.

4 Cook until patties are lightly golden and internal cooked temperature indicates 165°F (74°C) when measured with a meat thermometer.

5 To serve, spread raita on naan bread, add turkey patty and top with mango chutney.

TIPS Raita is a yogurt cucumber sauce seasoned with cumin. To make your own, combine 1 cup (250 mL) plain Greek-style yogurt with 1 tsp (5 mL) ground cumin, ½ English cucumber, diced, 1 tsp (5 mL) chopped fresh mint and salt and pepper to taste. It's best if it sits for 20 minutes for flavors to meld.

To cook only one burger, place tray in middle position of cooking chamber. Cook as directed above.

To avoid gluten, use gluten-free bread crumbs and naan bread.

NASHVILLE HOT TURKEY TENDERS

MAKES 4 SERVINGS

These fried turkey strips tossed in a dare-worthy chili mixture are addictively spicy, so get ready to sweat. Serve with simple white bread under the chicken to absorb the juices and flavors and pickles on top. I gave mine a twist, using turkey tenders, but if chicken tenders are all you can find, they are equally perfect.

PREP TIME
20 minutes

MARINATING TIME
3 hours or overnight

COOK TIME
12 minutes

VORTEX PROGRAMS
▶ **Air Fry**

2 tsp (10 mL) salt

1 tsp (5 mL) freshly ground black pepper

1 to 1½ tsp (5 to 7 mL) cayenne pepper, divided

2 tbsp (30 mL) hot sauce

2 lbs (1 kg) turkey tenderloins cut into 4- by 1-inch (10 by 2.5 cm) strips

1½ cups (375 mL) buttermilk

2 eggs, beaten

1 cup (250 mL) all-purpose flour

2 cups (500 mL) corn flakes crumbs

Hot sauce (such as Frank's RedHot)

Nonstick cooking spray

White bread slices

Bread and butter pickles

▶ SHALLOW BOWL OR SEALABLE BAG

1 In a shallow bowl or sealable freezer bag, combine salt, pepper, 1 tsp (5 mL) cayenne and hot sauce. Add turkey and toss with seasonings. Place in refrigerator for 3 hours or overnight

2 In a bowl, add buttermilk and eggs; whisk to combine. Add flour and remaining ½ tsp (2 mL) cayenne pepper; whisk or beat until no lumps remain. (Mixture will be very thick.) In a second bowl or shallow dish, place corn flakes crumbs. Add turkey to batter bowl, then transfer to crushed corn flakes and roll in crumbs to ensure each strip is completely covered.

3 Place turkey on cooking trays, allowing space between tenders to make sure nothing overlaps. Spray tenders on both sides with cooking spray. Let stand 10 minutes before cooking.

4 Place a drip pan in the bottom of the cooking chamber. Using the display panel, select **AIR FRY**, set **TEMPERATURE** to 375°F (190°C) and **TIME** to 12 minutes. **PREHEAT** Vortex until display indicates **ADD FOOD**.

5 Slide cooking trays into the bottom and middle positions. When display panel indicates **TURN FOOD**, switch cooking trays so that tray in top position moves to bottom position and bottom tray moves to top position.

6 Once cooked, remove turkey to a bowl and drizzle with more hot sauce. To serve, place turkey strips on a slice of white bread and garnish tops with pickles.

TIPS If you are sensitive to spicy food, have a cold glass of milk or a spoonful of yogurt on hand to take away the burning sensation. A protein called casein is present in dairy products that help to break up the hot sauce and offer some relief from its effects.

If you like it spicier, add more cayenne pepper to the batter.

OPEN-FACE TURKEY & AVOCADO SANDWICH

MAKES 4 SERVINGS

DF

This sandwich is so good, you are going to need a knife and fork to eat it. Long slender panini-style rolls are best to show off the layers of color.

PREP TIME
15 minutes

MARINATING TIME
30 minutes or up to
6 hours

COOK TIME
10 minutes

VORTEX PROGRAMS
▶ **Air Fry**
▶ **Broil**

---

3 tbsp (45 mL) freshly squeezed lime juice, divided

1 tbsp (15 mL) olive oil

½ tsp (2 mL) freshly ground black pepper

¼ tsp (1 mL) dried oregano

¼ tsp (1 mL) hot pepper flakes

4 skinless, boneless turkey breasts cutlets

2 panini rolls, sliced lengthwise

1 ripe avocado

Salt

2 tomatoes

½ red onion, thinly sliced

1 cup (250 mL) shredded Monterey Jack cheese

1 In a shallow dish, combine 2 tbsp (30 mL) lime juice, oil, pepper, oregano and hot pepper flakes. Add turkey cutlets and turn to coat evenly. Cover and marinate at room temperature for 30 minutes or in refrigerator for up to 6 hours.

2 Place turkey cutlets on one or two cooking trays, giving space between cutlets and not overlapping. Place drip pan in the bottom of the cooking chamber. Using the display panel, select **AIR FRY**, adjust **TEMPERATURE** to 400°F (200°C) and set **TIME** to 10 minutes. Press **START**. **PREHEAT** Vortex until display indicates **ADD FOOD**.

3 If using one tray, slide cooking tray into middle position. When display indicates **TURN FOOD**, turn cutlets over. If using two trays, slide into middle and bottom positions. When display indicates **TURN FOOD**, turn cutlets over and switch bottom tray to top position and middle tray to bottom position.

4 Cook until lightly browned, internal cooked temperature indicates 160°F (71°C) when measured with a meat thermometer and meat is no longer pink inside. Transfer to a plate; cover and keep warm.

5 Using the display panel, select **BROIL**, adjust **TEMPERATURE** to 400°F (200°C) and set **TIME** to 3 minutes. Press **START** and preheat Vortex until display indicates **ADD FOOD**.

6 Place panini rolls, cut side up, on one cooking tray. Slide into middle position and cook until lightly browned on top.

7 Meanwhile, peel and halve avocado lengthwise; remove pit. In a small bowl, mash half the avocado. Add remaining 1 tbsp (15 mL) lime juice and a pinch of salt. Slice remaining avocado, tomato and red onion.

8 To assemble, slice turkey into thin slices on a diagonal. Spread four bottom halves of rolls with mashed avocado mixture. Top with turkey. Layer with avocado, tomato and onion slices. Top with cheese. Lay on two cooking trays.

9 Meanwhile, using the display panel, select **BROIL**, adjust **TEMPERATURE** to 400°F (200°C) and set **TIME** to 3 minutes. Press **START** and preheat Vortex until display indicates **ADD FOOD**.

10 Place sandwiches on one cooking tray. Slide into middle position and cook until cheese melts. Serve warm.

TIPS If you can't find turkey cutlets, you can substitute chicken cutlets or skinless, boneless chicken breast, pounded to $\frac{1}{4}$-inch (0.5 cm) thickness.

If the avocado yields to firm, gentle pressure and it has a dark color, you know it's ripe and ready to eat. Don't go just by color, though; make sure it does not feel "mushy" to the touch.

"THIS SANDWICH IS SO GOOD, YOU ARE GOING TO NEED A KNIFE AND FORK TO EAT IT."

MAIN DISHES
SEAFOOD

BANG BANG SHRIMP

MAKES 4 SERVINGS

GF

Based on a popular restaurant appetizer menu item, these shrimp are crispy, creamy, sweet and spicy. The secret is in the sauce, which is made with mayonnaise, hot sauce and Sweet Thai Chili Sauce. Put a bowl of these out, and they will be gone in a flash.

COOK TIME
5 minutes

VORTEX PROGRAMS
▶ **Air Fry**
▶ **Broil**

1 lb (500 g) shrimp, uncooked, shells off, tails on and deveined

½ (125 mL) buttermilk

¾ cup (175 mL) cornstarch

½ cup (125 mL) mayonnaise

¼ cup (60 mL) Sweet Thai Chili Sauce

¼ tsp (1 mL) hot chili sauce (such as Sriracha)

Juice of 1 lime

1 tsp (5 mL) liquid honey

¼ tsp (1 mL) salt

Olive oil cooking spray

Chopped fresh cilantro

1 Place shrimp in a bowl; pour buttermilk over and let stand 20 minutes.

2 Place cornstarch in a bowl. Holding on to the tail, remove shrimp from the buttermilk, allowing excess buttermilk to drip away, then transfer into cornstarch. Coat each side of shrimp with cornstarch, then lay on two cooking trays. Spray with cooking spray.

3 Place the drip pan in the bottom of the cooking chamber. Using the display panel, select **AIR FRY**, adjust **TEMPERATURE** to 400°F (200°C) and set **TIME** for 7 minutes. Press **START**. **PREHEAT** Vortex until display indicates **ADD FOOD**.

4 Insert one cooking tray in the top position and the other tray in the bottom position. Close the door. When display indicates **TURN FOOD**, turn shrimp over and switch trays so bottom tray moves to top position and middle tray moves to bottom position.

5 Meanwhile, in a medium bowl, combine mayonnaise, Sweet Thai Chili Sauce, hot sauce, lime juice, honey and salt.

6 Add shrimp to bowl with mayonnaise and toss to coat. Place shrimps back on cooking trays. Using display panel, select **BROIL**, set **TEMPERATURE** to 400°F (200°C) and **TIME** to 2 minutes. **PREHEAT** Vortex until display indicates **ADD FOOD**.

7 Cook until lightly browned on top. Garnish with chopped fresh cilantro.

TIPS You can skip the broiling step and just enjoy the shrimp tossed in the sauce.

I recommend using peeled shrimp, but I like the tails on, so I tend to purchase shrimp with the shells on and peel them myself, leaving the tails intact.

Substitute Greek yogurt for the mayonnaise if you wish.

SWEET THAI CHILI SAUCE
MAKES 4 TO 6 SERVINGS

You can purchase a store-bought chili sauce or make your own Sweet Thai Chili Sauce. I keep leftover sauce in a sealed jar in the refrigerator.

1 cup (250 mL) rice wine vinegar

¾ cup (175 mL) granulated sugar

2 tbsp (30 mL) chili paste (such as sambal oelek)

1 tbsp (15 mL) fish sauce

1 tbsp (15 mL) minced gingerroot

1 tbsp (15 mL) minced garlic

½ tsp (2 mL) salt

1 To make your own Sweet Thai Chili Sauce, combine rice wine vinegar, sugar, chili paste and fish sauce. Bring mixture to a boil, reduce heat and simmer 10 to 15 minutes until slightly thickened and reduced by half. Add minced ginger, minced garlic and salt.

BLACKENED FISH TACOS
WITH MANGO SLAW

MAKES 4 TO 6 SERVINGS

This marinated, spiced and blackened fish tastes delicious wrapped in a warm corn tortilla with the crunchy Mango Slaw. The combination of flavors and textures make them hard to resist. I like them with a slice of avocado too.

PREP TIME
20 minutes

MARINATING TIME
1 hour for slaw,
30 minutes for fish

COOK TIME
8 to 10 minutes

VORTEX PROGRAMS
▶ Air Fry

MANGO SLAW

2 cups (500 mL) prepared coleslaw mix

1 mango, peeled and diced

Juice of 1 lime

1 tbsp (15 mL) mayonnaise

Salt and freshly ground black pepper to taste

BLACKENED FISH TACOS

½ lb (250 g) frozen white fish fillets such as haddock, tilapia or mahi mahi, thawed

Juice of one lime

1 tsp (5 mL) hot sauce

continued →

1 *Mango Slaw:* In a bowl, combine coleslaw mix, mango, lime juice and mayonnaise; toss until well combined. Cover and refrigerate for 1 hour.

2 *Blackened Fish Tacos:* Place fish in a shallow baking pan. In a small bowl, combine lime juice, hot sauce, smoked paprika, garlic powder and pepper. Coat both sides of fish with marinade, cover and refrigerate for 30 minutes.

3 Lay fish fillets out onto cooking trays, ensuring there is enough space around the fillets. Spray each side of fillets with cooking spray.

4 Place drip pan in the bottom of the cooking chamber. Using the display panel, select **AIR FRY**, then adjust **TEMPERATURE** to 380°F (193°C) and set **TIME** to 10 minutes. Press **START** to preheat.

5 When display panel indicates **ADD FOOD**, place one tray in the top position and the other in the bottom position. Air fry until display panel indicates **TURN FOOD**.

6 Using a spatula, turn fish over and switch trays around so that top tray moves to the bottom position and bottom tray moves to top position. Continue to cook, ensuring fish flakes easily with a fork when done.

7 To assemble fish tacos, divide the fish among the six warmed tortilla shells. Top with Mango Slaw and fresh cilantro. Serve with lime wedges.

1 tsp (5 mL) smoked paprika

1 tsp (5 mL) garlic powder

1 tsp (5 mL) freshly ground black pepper

Nonstick cooking spray

Six 6-inch (15 cm) corn or flour tortillas, warmed

Fresh cilantro

Lime wedges

TIPS Store any leftover fish and slaw in separate containers in the refrigerator for up to 3 days.

I find it easy to use a bag of prepared coleslaw mix for making slaw. It has red and green cabbage plus grated carrots too. Then I add extras like red and green onions for a flavor boost.

"THIS MARINATED, SPICED AND BLACKENED FISH TASTES DELICIOUS WRAPPED IN A WARM CORN TORTILLA WITH THE CRUNCHY MANGO SLAW."

EAST COAST CRAB CAKES
WITH EASY AÏOLI

MAKES 4 SERVINGS

My husband will do just about anything to get his hands on some crab cakes. They are always in the appetizer sections of fancy seafood restaurants, so it might seem like they are intimidating to make, but truly they are so simple, literally anyone can make them — even my husband.

PREP TIME
10 minutes

COOK TIME
10 minutes

VORTEX PROGRAMS
▶ **Air Fry**

EAST COAST CRAB CAKES

¼ cup (60 mL) mayonnaise

1 tsp (5 mL) Dijon mustard

1 tsp (5 mL) Worcestershire sauce

½ tsp (2 mL) salt

¼ tsp (1 mL) freshly ground black pepper

1 lb (500 g) crabmeat, thawed if frozen

1 cup (250 mL) fresh bread crumbs

3 green onions, chopped

1 red bell pepper, seeded and finely chopped

¼ cup (60 mL) chopped fresh parsley

Olive oil cooking spray

continued →

1 *East Coast Crab Cakes:* In a small bowl, mix together mayonnaise, mustard, Worcestershire, salt and pepper.

2 In a medium bowl, stir together crabmeat, bread crumbs, green onions, bell pepper and parsley. Fold in mayonnaise mixture; mix well and shape into four large or eight smaller patties. Set onto two cooking trays and spray with cooking spray.

3 Place drip pan in the bottom of the cooking chamber. Using the display panel, select **AIR FRY**, adjust **TEMPERATURE** to 400°F (200°C) and set **TIME** for 10 minutes then select **START**. **PREHEAT** Vortex until display indicates **ADD FOOD**.

4 Slide trays into bottom and top positions. When display indicates **TURN FOOD**, flip crab cakes over and switch bottom tray to top position and top tray to bottom position. Cook until golden. Serve with lemon wedges and Easy Aïoli.

5 *Easy Aïoli:* In a bowl, combine mayonnaise, garlic and lemon juice. Let stand 10 minutes for flavors to meld.

EASY AÏOLI

¼ cup (60 mL) mayonnaise

2 cloves garlic, grated

1 tsp (5 mL) freshly
squeezed lemon juice

Lemon wedges

TIPS Mayonnaise is the perfect binder, and its subtle creaminess won't compete with the crab — in fact, it helps it shine. If you are not a fan of mayonnaise, Greek yogurt is a great alternative.

The Dijon mustard and Worcestershire sauce help to wake up the flavor of the crab cakes. If you like a little more zip, add a few dashes of hot sauce to the crabmeat mixture.

To reheat, place cooking tray in the middle position. On the display panel, select **REHEAT**, set **TEMPERATURE** to 350°F (180°C) and **TIME** for 5 minutes.

CURRIED APPLE & TUNA MELT

MAKES 2 SERVINGS

A tuna melt takes me back to my university years, when I didn't have much money for groceries and a can of tuna was an inexpensive protein source. However, this version is all dressed and grown up. Skip the cheese on the top if you want to go dairy free. It's just as good without.

PREP TIME
20 minutes

COOK TIME
8 minutes

VORTEX PROGRAMS

▹ Bake

▹ Air Fry

1 can (7 oz/170 g) tuna

1 stalk celery, finely chopped

2 green onions, white and green parts, finely chopped

1 Granny Smith apple, cored and chopped

1 tbsp (15 mL) chopped fresh parsley

2 tsp (10 mL) fresh lemon juice

1 tsp (5 mL) curry powder

3 tbsp (45 mL) mayonnaise

2 slices hearty grain bread or naan

2 slices Provolone cheese (optional)

1 Drain tuna and place in a bowl. Add celery, green onions, apple, parsley, lemon juice, curry powder and mayonnaise; mix well to combine.

2 Divide mixture evenly onto bread slices. Place on cooking tray. Place drip pan in the bottom of the cooking chamber. Using the display panel, select BAKE, adjust TEMPERATURE to 400°F (200°C) and set TIME to 6 minutes. Press START. PREHEAT Vortex until display indicates ADD FOOD.

3 Slide cooking tray into middle position. Ignore display when it indicates TURN FOOD, and continue to cook until tuna is hot.

4 Remove from cooking chamber and top with cheese. Reset Vortex to AIR FRY, adjust TEMPERATURE to 400°F (200°C) and set TIME to 2 minutes. When display indicates ADD FOOD, slide tray into middle position. Cook until cheese is bubbly and hot.

TIPS When a recipe calls for green onions, some people only use the "green" part and not the white. I always use both parts so I have a mixture of color and texture.

You can use any good melting cheese for the top of these tuna melts — Cheddar, Monterey Jack or mozzarella are all good options.

FISH-IN-CHIPS SANDWICH

MAKES 4 SERVINGS

Of course you can't have fish without chips, but what about fish coated in potato chips? Is that not a win-win? Potato chips are already seasoned and when they are crumbled they make the perfect crust for the fish fillets.

PREP TIME
10 minutes

COOK TIME
12 to 15 minutes

VORTEX PROGRAMS
▶ **Air Fry**
▶ **Broil**

¼ cup (60 mL) mayonnaise

1 tsp (5 mL) Dijon mustard

1 tsp (5 mL) lemon juice

4 cod fillets, about 6 oz (175 g) each, thawed if frozen

1 cup (250 mL) finely crushed plain potato chips, preferably lightly salted

4 hamburger buns, regular or gluten-free

4 Cheddar cheese slices (optional)

Tartar sauce

Shredded romaine lettuce

1 In a small bowl, combine mayonnaise, mustard and lemon juice. Brush over all sides of each fish fillet. Roll or press fillet into potato chips, coating all sides of fillet. Lay on cooking tray.

2 Place drip pan in the bottom of cooking chamber. Using the display panel, select **AIR FRY**, adjust **TEMPERATURE** to 350°F (180°C) and set **TIME** to 12 to 14 minutes, depending on the thickness of the fish. **PREHEAT** Vortex until display indicates **ADD FOOD**.

3 If using one tray, place cooking tray in the middle position. If using two trays, place in bottom and middle positions. When display indicates **TURN FOOD**, flip fillets over and switch bottom cooking tray to top position and middle cooking tray to bottom position. Cook until opaque and fish flakes easily with a fork.

4 Place cheese slice, if using, on bottom half of bun. Place buns on one cooking tray. Using the display panel, select **BROIL**, adjust **TEMPERATURE** to 400°F (200°C) and set **TIME** to 2 minutes. **PREHEAT** Vortex until display indicates **ADD FOOD**. **BROIL** until cheese is melted and top half of bun is golden.

5 To assemble, lay fish fillet over melted cheese. Top with tartar sauce and shredded lettuce and other half of bun. Serve warm.

TIPS You can use frozen, thawed fillets for this recipe. I tested it with both frozen cod and haddock, and both were excellent. Add a little more cooking time, depending on the thickness of your fillets.

To safely thaw frozen fish, place the fish in the refrigerator overnight so it can thaw out gradually. This way you will preserve the fish's flavor and texture. If you need to thaw quickly, keep fish in its vacuum-sealed package (or place into a sealable bag). Submerge fish in a pot of cold water for about an hour.

JALAPEÑO LIME CRUSTED HALIBUT

MAKES 4 SERVINGS

A simple crust makes this halibut recipe super easy to prepare, but the results taste sublime. While halibut is what I call "steak of the sea," you can also put this topping on any type of fish such as salmon, trout, haddock or cod.

PREP TIME

10 minutes

COOK TIME

12 minutes

VORTEX PROGRAM

▶ **Roast**

½ cup (125 mL) mayonnaise

Zest and juice of 1 lime

1 tbsp (15 mL) chopped jalapeño pepper

Four 6-oz (175 g) fillets halibut or other firm fish, thawed if frozen

1 tbsp (15 mL) grated Parmesan cheese

1 In a bowl, combine mayonnaise, zest and juice of lime, and jalapeño. Evenly divide mayonnaise mixture over top of each fish fillet. Sprinkle with cheese.

2 Place drip pan in the bottom of cooking chamber. Using the display panel, select **ROAST**, adjust **TEMPERATURE** to 350°F (180°C) and set **TIME** to 12 to 14 minutes depending on the thickness of the fish. **PREHEAT** Vortex until display indicates **ADD FOOD**.

3 If using one cooking tray, place tray in the middle position. If using two trays, place in bottom and middle racks. When display indicates **TURN FOOD**, switch bottom cooking tray to top position and middle tray to bottom position. Cook until browned on top, fish is opaque inside and easily flakes with a fork.

TIPS To safely thaw frozen fish, place the fish in the refrigerator overnight so it can thaw out gradually. This way you will preserve the fish's flavor and texture. If you need to thaw quickly, keep fish in its vacuum-sealed package (or place into a sealable bag). Submerge fish in a pot of cold water for about an hour.

MAPLE MISO SALMON

MAKES 3 TO 4 SERVINGS

This simple glaze combines salty and savory miso paste with sweet maple syrup. The rice vinegar marries the two in this very simple but sophisticated dish. Serve over steamed rice with a little pan-fried or steamed bok choy.

PREP TIME

5 minutes

COOK TIME

7 to 9 minutes

VORTEX PROGRAMS

▶ **Air Fry**

▶ **Broil (optional)**

2 tbsp (30 mL) yellow miso paste

2 tbsp (30 mL) rice wine vinegar

2 tbsp (30 mL) maple syrup

1 tsp (5 mL) sesame oil

1¼ lb (625 g) salmon fillet, skin on

1 In a bowl, combine miso paste, vinegar, maple syrup and sesame oil. Place salmon on cooking tray and brush with miso mixture.

2 Place drip pan in the bottom of the cooking chamber. Pour water into the bottom of the drip pan.

3 Using the display panel, select **AIR FRY**, adjust **TEMPERATURE** to 375°F (190°C) and set **TIME** for 8 minutes then select **START**. **PREHEAT** Vortex until display indicates **ADD FOOD**.

4 Place cooking tray in the middle position. When display indicates **TURN FOOD**, turn cooking tray around front to back and cook until opaque and fish flakes easily with a fork.

5 Remove tray and let salmon rest. Set Vortex to **BROIL**, set **TEMPERATURE** to 400°F (200°C) and **TIME** to 2 minutes. When display indicates **ADD FOOD**, slide tray into middle position. **BROIL** until glazed and glistening on top, if desired.

TIPS I prefer to leave the skin on the salmon. First of all, it's so tasty. It also provides a safety layer between the fish's flesh and the hot cooking pan.

Miso is a fermented soybean paste that adds a salty umami flavor to many Japanese dishes. It has a similar texture to peanut butter and comes in different colors. White or light miso is light beige to yellow in color and tends to be lighter and sweeter in flavor because of a shorter fermentation. Red or dark miso ranges from light brown to almost black. I prefer the lighter miso, but I have also made it with a red miso and it is just as delicious.

MAIN DISHES
MEATLESS

FAST & EASY PIZZA CRUST

MAKES 2 TO 4 SERVINGS

This pizza crust comes together so quickly you will have fresh homemade pizza within an hour. Choose your own toppings. I especially love how the air fry function cooks cheese just like it comes on pizzeria pizza.

PREP TIME

15 minutes

PROOF TIME

30 minutes

COOK TIME

8 minutes

VORTEX PROGRAMS

▸ **Proof**

▸ **Air Fry**

Olive oil cooking spray

Yellow cornmeal

½ cup (125 mL) warm water

1 tbsp (15 mL) active dry yeast

1 tsp (5 mL) granulated sugar

1 ½ cups (375 mL) all-purpose flour

¼ tsp (1 mL) salt

1 tbsp (15 mL) olive oil

1 Spray one cooking tray with olive oil cooking spray, then sprinkle cornmeal over; set aside.

2 In a small bowl, mix warm water with yeast and sugar. Let stand 5 minutes until yeast activates and mixture looks frothy.

3 In a large bowl, mix together flour and salt. Pour in activated yeast mixture and oil and stir together until a shaggy dough forms. Turn out onto counter and knead about 10 minutes until smooth dough is achieved.

4 Press or roll dough out into a rectangle the same size as the cooking tray. Place into prepared cooking tray and rub top with a light coating of olive oil. Place in Vortex and close door.

5 Select **PROOF** (90°F /32°C) and set **TIME** for 30 minutes.

6 Once dough is proofed, remove from cooking chamber. Add your favorite toppings. See Tip, below.

7 Place drip pan in the bottom of the cooking chamber. Close door. Select **AIR FRY**, adjust **TEMPERATURE** to 400°F (200°C) and set **TIME** to 8 minutes. When Vortex indicates **ADD FOOD**, slide cooking tray into the bottom or middle position. Cook until crust is golden and cheese is melted and bubbly.

TIPS I worked through a lot of pizza dough to get this recipe just right for the Vortex. If you don't have a **PROOF** function, just leave it to proof for 1 hour on the counter.

Try these topping options: Marinated artichokes, broccoli florets, red bell pepper slices, sun-dried tomato slivers, plum (Roma) tomato slices, pitted black olives, sliced mushrooms, crumbled feta cheese or grated mozzarella cheese. For meat lovers, try bacon, pancetta or crumbled cooked Italian sausage.

FLATBREAD RICOTTA PESTO PIZZA
WITH ROASTED VEGGIES

MAKES 2 SERVINGS

"Let's order pizza!" The next time you hear those words, instead of ordering in, assemble these ingredients to make your own gourmet pizzas. It's so easy with store-bought flatbreads that fit perfectly on the cooking trays.

PREP TIME
20 minutes

COOK TIME
5 minutes + 6 minutes

VORTEX PROGRAMS
▶ Air Fry

---

1 small onion, chopped

½ red bell pepper, seeded and chopped

Nonstick cooking spray

2 prebaked 8-inch (20 cm) flatbreads, such as Greek-style pitas or naan bread

3 tbsp (45 mL) prepared pesto

½ cup (125 mL) ricotta cheese

½ cup (125 mL) chopped broccoli florets

2 tbsp (30 mL) freshly grated Parmesan cheese

¼ tsp (1 mL) dried oregano

Salt and freshly ground black pepper

1 Place onion and bell pepper on drip pan and spray with cooking spray.

2 Using the display panel, select **AIR FRY**, adjust **TEMPERATURE** to 350°F (180°C) and set **TIME** to 5 minutes. Press **START**. **PREHEAT** Vortex until display indicates **ADD FOOD**.

3 Slide drip pan into middle position in cooking chamber. When display indicates **TURN FOOD**, stir vegetables. Cook until tender and onions are translucent. Remove from cooking chamber and cool.

4 Place flatbreads on two cooking trays. Spread with half the pesto. Dot the tops with ricotta cheese. Sprinkle with chopped broccoli and cooked vegetables. Drizzle with remaining pesto and sprinkle with Parmesan cheese and oregano. Season with salt and pepper. Lightly spray each pizza with cooking spray.

5 Using the display panel, select **AIR FRY**, adjust **TEMPERATURE** to 375°F (190°C) and set **TIME** to 6 minutes. Press **START**. **PREHEAT** Vortex until display indicates **ADD FOOD**.

6 Slide cooking trays into top and bottom positions. When display indicates **TURN FOOD**, move top tray to bottom position and bottom tray to top position. Cook until cheese is melted and pizzas are lightly browned.

TIPS This recipe is the perfect way to use up odd bits of vegetables and deli meats you have left in the refrigerator. Vary the toppings according to what you have.

You can also make these pizzas on four split English muffins. Arrange two split muffins per cooking tray.

HERBED FALAFELS
WITH LEMON TAHINI SAUCE

MAKES ABOUT 15 TO 16 FALAFELS

Falafels are a Middle Eastern treat made with chickpeas, parsley and seasonings. Shaped into little balls, they cook up well in the Vortex. You can serve them in a pita or wrap with shredded lettuce, tomatoes and cucumbers. Or forget the bread and just serve them as part of a salad. I like this Lemon Tahini Sauce, but a store-bought hummus, baba ghanouj or tzatziki are perfect accompaniments.

PREP TIME
15 minutes

COOK TIME
16 minutes

VORTEX PROGRAMS
▶ Air Fry

HERBED FALAFELS

1 can (19 oz/540 mL) chickpeas, drained and rinsed

1 medium onion, chopped

¼ cup (60 mL) chopped parsley

2 cloves garlic, minced

1 tsp (5 mL) ground cumin

1 tsp (5 mL) ground coriander

2 tbsp (30 mL) chickpea flour or all-purpose flour

1 tsp (5 mL) salt

½ tsp (2 mL) freshly ground black pepper

Nonstick cooking spray

continued →

▶ FOOD PROCESSOR OR BLENDER

1 Place drained chickpeas on a paper towel–lined baking tray and pat off any excess moisture. Place chickpeas in a food processor and add onion, parsley, garlic, cumin, coriander, chickpea flour, salt and pepper. Pulse until the mixture is coarse but not too mushy.

2 Scoop out 2 tbsp (30 mL) of mixture and shape into a round ball. Repeat until you have about 15 falafel balls. Place on two cooking trays and spray with cooking spray all over.

3 Using display panel, select **AIR FRY**, set **TEMPERATURE** to 400°F (200°C) and set **TIME** to 16 minutes. Press **START** to preheat.

4 When Vortex displays **ADD FOOD**, slide one tray into top position and other tray into bottom position. Cook until display indicates **TURN FOOD**.

5 Open door and transfer tray that was in top position to bottom and bottom tray to top. Cook until browned and crisp. Allow patties to cool for a few minutes before serving.

6 *Lemon Tahini Sauce:* In a small bowl, whisk together tahini and lemon juice. Slowly whisk in water to thin the sauce until it can drizzle from a spoon. (Add a bit more water if you need to thin it down more). Stir in garlic, salt, pepper and parsley, if desired. Serve over falafels.

LEMON TAHINI SAUCE

¼ cup (60 mL) tahini

2 tbsp (30 mL) freshly squeezed lemon juice

2 tbsp (30 mL) water

1 clove garlic, minced

½ tsp (2 mL) salt

¼ tsp (1 mL) freshly ground black pepper

1 tbsp (15 mL) chopped fresh parsley (optional)

TIPS Tahini is a paste made from sesame seeds and is a staple in many cuisines, especially in the Mediterranean and Middle East.

Chickpea flour is naturally gluten free and is sold in the international aisle and Middle Eastern grocery stores. It's commonly called besan. If you can't find it, you can substitute regular or gluten-free all-purpose flour.

I like to use a medium-size cookie scoop to measure out the falafels. That way I get consistent, even sizes.

If you find your falafel is falling apart, you can add a little more flour to help hold it together.

"FALAFELS ARE A MIDDLE EASTERN TREAT MADE WITH CHICKPEAS, PARSLEY AND SEASONINGS."

MEXICALI QUINOA STUFFED PEPPERS

MAKES 4 SERVINGS

These peppers are hearty, filling and oh-so-flavorful. The filling is loaded with quinoa, Mexican-inspired spices, black beans and corn, but becomes even more delectable when you stuff it into the peppers and roast them in the Vortex. Extra bonus — they are full of protein and fiber, plus vegan and gluten free.

PREP TIME
10 minutes

COOK TIME
16 minutes

VORTEX PROGRAM
▶ Air Fry

MEXICALI QUINOA STUFFED PEPPERS

1 cup (250 mL) cooked quinoa

¼ cup (60 mL) salsa

1 tsp (5 mL) ground cumin

½ tsp (2 mL) chili powder

½ tsp (2 mL) garlic powder

1 cup (250 mL) canned black beans, rinsed and drained

½ cup (125 mL) corn kernels, thawed if frozen

Salt and freshly ground black pepper

4 red, yellow or orange bell peppers

Olive oil cooking spray

1 ripe avocado, sliced

continued →

▶ BLENDER OR FOOD PROCESSOR

1 *Mexicali Quinoa Stuffed Peppers:* In a bowl, combine cooked quinoa, salsa, cumin, chili powder and garlic powder, black beans and corn. Mix to combine and season with salt and pepper to taste.

2 Cut a thin slice from stem end of each bell pepper to remove the top of the pepper. Remove seeds and membranes; rinse peppers. If necessary, cut a thin slice from the bottom of each pepper so they stand straight. Place peppers on one cooking tray. Spray peppers with cooking spray. Stuff peppers with quinoa mixture and spray the tops of stuffing.

3 Place drip pan in the bottom of the cooking chamber. Using the display panel, select **AIR FRY**, adjust **TEMPERATURE** to 380°F (193°C) and set **TIME** to 20 minutes. Press **START**. **PREHEAT** Vortex until display indicates **ADD FOOD**.

4 Slide cooking tray into middle position. When display indicates **TURN FOOD**, turn tray around in the cooking chamber back to front. Cook until peppers are tender and filling is heated through. Serve with sliced avocado and drizzle with Creamy Avocado Dressing.

5 *Creamy Avocado Dressing:* In a blender or food processor, combine avocado, cilantro, lime juice and cumin. Slowly pour in avocado oil and blend until completely emulsified. Season to taste with salt.

CREAMY AVOCADO DRESSING

½ ripe avocado

1 cup (250 mL) roughly chopped fresh cilantro

Juice of 2 limes (about ¼ cup/60 mL)

¼ tsp (1 mL) ground cumin

⅓ cup (75 mL) avocado or olive oil

Salt

TIPS To prepare quinoa: Place ½ cup (125 mL) quinoa in a fine mesh strainer and thoroughly rinse and drain well. In a small pot, combine quinoa and 1 cup (250 mL) water (or vegetable stock). Bring to a boil, reduce heat, cover and simmer on low until all the liquid is absorbed and quinoa is fluffy, about 20 minutes.

PORTOBELLO BARLEY BURGERS

MAKES 4

These barley burgers were a huge hit for lunch when I served them to a bridal party with vegetarians. Now I serve them whenever I want a change from regular burgers. I like whole wheat or grainy dinner rolls, but you could skip the carbs and serve it on a bed of salad greens. But don't miss out on the onion jam!

PREP TIME

20 minutes

COOK TIME

12 + 6 minutes

VORTEX PROGRAMS

▸ **Roast**

▸ **Air Fry**

▸ **Toast**

MARINADE

1½ tbsp (20 mL) maple syrup

1 tbsp (15 mL) apple cider vinegar

1 tsp (5 mL) minced garlic

½ tsp (2 mL) salt

½ tsp (2 mL) freshly ground black pepper

PORTOBELLO BARLEY BURGERS

2 portobello mushroom caps

Olive oil cooking spray

1 egg

1½ cups (375 mL) cooked barley

¼ cup (60 mL) dry bread crumbs

continued →

▸ FOOD PROCESSOR

1 *Marinade:* In a cup, combine maple syrup, vinegar, garlic, salt and pepper.

2 *Portobello Barley Burgers:* Place drip pan in the bottom of the cooking chamber. Using the display panel, select ROAST, adjust TEMPERATURE to 350°F (180°C) and set TIME to 12 minutes. Press START. PREHEAT Vortex until display indicates ADD FOOD. Spray tops of mushrooms with cooking spray, then lay them on cooking tray, stem side up, and drizzle marinade over.

3 Roast until tender. Remove and let cool. Chop once cool enough to handle.

4 In a food processor, combine mushrooms, egg, ¼ cup (60 mL) cooked barley, bread crumbs, flour and thyme leaves. Pulse to combine, leaving slightly chunky. Transfer mixture to a bowl. Add remaining 1¼ cup (300 mL) cooked barley, and shredded kale. Shape mixture into four burgers. Place burgers on cooking tray and lightly spray with cooking spray

5 Using the display panel, select AIR FRY, adjust TEMPERATURE to 380°F (180°C) and set TIME to 6 minutes. Press START. PREHEAT Vortex until display indicates ADD FOOD. Slide tray into middle position and cook until heated through and thermometer registers 165°F (74°C).

6 Toast buns. Using display panel, select TOAST and use preset L2 (3:10 minutes) and lightly toast buns. Spread bottom of buns with onion jam. Top with burger, crumbled goat's cheese and radish sprouts.

¼ cup (60 mL) all-purpose flour

1 tsp (5 mL) dried thyme

½ cup (125 mL) shredded kale leaves

Whole wheat buns

GARNISHES

Crumbled goat's cheese, radish sprouts, onion jam

TIPS To cook barley: Rinse ¾ cup (175 mL) barley well under cold running water. Transfer to a pot and cover with cold water, ensuring water is 1 inch (2.5 cm) above the barley. Bring mixture to a boil, reduce heat, cover and cook on low for 15 to 18 minutes or until tender. Remove from heat, drain and cool.

Onion jam is available in the condiment section of good grocery stores or gourmet food shops. Good chutney is another great option too. It's that sweet and savory combination you are looking for here.

"THESE BARLEY BURGERS WERE A HUGE HIT FOR LUNCH WHEN I SERVED THEM TO A BRIDAL PARTY WITH VEGETARIANS."

ROASTED HALOUMI & SWEET POTATOES WITH CHIMICHURRI

MAKES 4 SERVINGS

GF

The salty squeak of haloumi is one of my favorite things. Combine it with herby chimichurri and roasted veggies to make this dish a triple treat! I eat it as a main dish, but you can also serve it as a side dish.

PREP TIME
15 minutes

COOK TIME
35 minutes

VORTEX PROGRAMS

▶ Roast

▶ Air Fry

CHIMICHURRI

¼ cup (60 mL) chopped fresh cilantro

¼ cup (60 mL) chopped fresh parsley

2 cloves garlic, minced

1 lemon, zested and juiced

½ tsp (2 mL) hot pepper flakes

ROASTED HALOUMI AND SWEET POTATOES

¼ cup (60 mL) olive oil

4 tsp (20 mL) ground cumin

2 medium sweet potatoes, washed and chopped into 1-inch (2.5 cm) cubes

continued →

1 *Chimichurri:* In a bowl, combine cilantro, parsley, garlic, lemon zest, lemon juice and hot pepper flakes; mix well and set aside.

2 *Roasted Haloumi and Sweet Potatoes:* In a bowl, mix together ¼ cup (60 mL) olive oil and 4 tsp (20 mL) ground cumin; set aside.

3 In a large bowl, toss sweet potatoes with 2 tbsp (30 mL) of the cumin oil and spread onto two cooking trays. Season with salt and pepper. Toss red onion in 1 tbsp (15 mL) cumin oil; set aside.

4 Place the drip pan into the bottom of the cooking chamber. Using the display panel, select **ROAST**, adjust **TEMPERATURE** to 350°F (180°C) and set **TIME** to 30 minutes. **PREHEAT** Vortex until display indicates **ADD FOOD**.

5 Slide cooking trays into the middle and bottom positions. Cook sweet potatoes until display panel indicates **TURN FOOD**. Slide trays out and add red onion evenly to both cooking trays. Toss vegetables together. Switch bottom tray to top position and middle tray to bottom position. Continue to cook until vegetables are golden brown and potatoes are tender.

6 Remove cooking trays from cooking chamber and transfer cooked vegetables to a bowl. Add tomatoes and avocado and toss together; set aside.

7 Meanwhile, toss haloumi cubes in remaining cumin oil, then lay cubes onto cooking tray.

Salt and freshly ground black pepper

1 red onion, coarsely chopped

½ cup (125 mL) grape tomatoes, cut in half lengthwise

1 avocado, cubed

1 package (160 g) haloumi, cut into 1-inch (2.5 cm) cubes

8 Using display panel, select **AIR FRY**, adjust **TEMPERATURE** to 350°F (180°C) and set **TIME** to 5 minutes. **PREHEAT** Vortex until display indicates **ADD FOOD**. Cook haloumi until golden brown and softened. Add to bowl with sweet potatoes.

9 To serve, transfer vegetable mixture onto serving plate and drizzle with chimichurri. Season with salt and pepper to taste.

TIPS Haloumi is a semi-hard, brined cheese made from a mixture of goat's and sheep's cheese. Because it has a high melting point, it can easily be grilled or fried. It's an excellent choice for the Vortex. I lay the cubes directly on the cooking tray and watch them get soft and melty as they air fry.

If you don't have time to make the Chimichurri from scratch, feel free to use a premade sauce. However, I like to double this recipe and keep extra in the refrigerator so it's ready at hand for lots of different dishes.

If you're not a fan of cilantro, fresh chopped oregano makes an excellent substitute.

THE BEYOND AMAZING NACHO BURGER

MAKES 4 SERVINGS

Plant-based burgers are becoming quite popular and can be found in the fresh meat counters next to meat burgers. They are a great choice for the Vortex too. While they are cooking, prep some guacamole and make this plant-friendly nacho sauce, and you have a recipe for an amazing twist on a burger.

PREP TIME
15 minutes

COOK TIME
10 minutes

VORTEX PROGRAMS
▶ Air Fry

NOT-SO-NACHO CHEESE SAUCE

2 tbsp (30 mL) chopped shallots

1 cup (250 mL) chopped yellow potatoes, unpeeled

¼ cup (60 mL) chopped carrot (about 1 small)

⅓ cup (75 mL) chopped onion

1 cup (250 mL) water

2 slices bread, torn into large pieces

6 tbsp (90 mL) plant-based butter-type spread, divided

¼ tsp (1 mL) paprika

¼ cup (60 mL) soaked raw cashews, drained

2 tsp (10 mL) sea salt

continued →

▶ FOOD PROCESSOR

1 *Not-So-Nacho Cheese Sauce:* In a medium saucepan, combine shallots, potatoes, carrots, onion and water. Bring vegetables to a boil, reduce heat and simmer covered, for 15 minutes, or until vegetables are very soft.

2 Meanwhile in a food processor fitted with a metal blade, add bread, 1 tbsp (15 mL) butter and paprika; process until combined to a medium-fine texture, set aside.

3 Place cashews, salt, garlic, remaining butter, mustard, lemon juice, black pepper, and cayenne to food processor. Add the softened vegetables and cooking water and process until perfectly smooth.

4 *Beyond Amazing Nacho Burgers:* Place burgers on one or two cooking trays. Sprinkle with seasoned salt and lightly spray with cooking spray. Place drip pan in the bottom of cooking chamber. Using the display panel, select **AIR FRY**, adjust **TEMPERATURE** to 375°F (190°C) and set **TIME** to 10 minutes. **PREHEAT** Vortex until display indicates **ADD FOOD**.

5 If cooking only two burgers, use one cooking tray, placing tray in middle position. When display indicates **TURN FOOD**, flip patties over. If using two trays, place cooking trays in bottom and middle positions. When display indicates **TURN FOOD**, flip patties over and switch bottom cooking tray to top position and middle cooking tray to bottom position. Cook until lightly browned, juices run clear when pierced and internal temperature reads 165°F (74°C) on meat thermometer.

¼ tsp (1 mL) garlic, minced (about 1 medium clove)

¼ tsp (1 mL) Dijon mustard

1 tbsp (15 mL) freshly squeezed lemon juice (optional)

¼ tsp (1 mL) freshly ground black pepper

Pinch cayenne pepper

BEYOND AMAZING NACHO BURGERS

4 plant-based burgers

Seasoned salt

Olive oil cooking spray

4 sesame seed buns, split in half

1 cup (250 mL) tortilla chips

Shredded lettuce

¼ cup (60 mL) salsa

6 To assemble, place patty on bottom of bun, then top with lettuce, salsa, tortilla chips, and nacho sauce. Spread top bun with guacamole and place over burger.

TIPS Rather than using store-bought guacamole, make your own. Combine 1 mashed avocado, juice of ½ lime and season to taste with salt.

You can make the Not-So-Nacho sauce up to 3 days in advance. Store in the refrigerator. Reheat in microwave for 2 minutes.

SPINACH SALAD WITH CRISPY TOFU

MAKES 4 SERVINGS

A hearty salad of baby spinach and crispy tofu is great for lunch or a light weeknight dinner. The trick to getting crispy tofu is to drain the tofu and weight it down for 30 minutes. The few extra steps of preparation are worth the effort.

PREP TIME
20 minutes

MARINATING TIME
30 minutes + 30 minutes

COOK TIME
25 minutes

VORTEX PROGRAM
▶ **Air Fry**

SOY CIDER DRESSING

1 tbsp (15 mL) nutritional yeast flakes

1½ tbsp (20 mL) water

1½ tbsp (20 mL) soy sauce

1½ tbsp (20 mL) apple cider vinegar

1 clove garlic, crushed

1 tbsp (15 mL) tahini

¼ cup (60 mL) vegetable oil

SPINACH SALAD WITH CRISPY TOFU

1 package (350 g) firm tofu, cut into ½-inch (1 cm) slices, pressed

2 tbsp (30 mL) soy sauce

2 tsp (10 mL) sesame oil

1 tbsp (15 mL) rice wine vinegar

continued →

▶ BLENDER OR FOOD PROCESSOR

1 *Soy Cider Dressing:* In a blender or food processor, combine yeast flakes, water, soy sauce, apple cider vinegar, garlic and tahini; process until smooth. Add vegetable oil in a steady stream and blend until completely incorporated. Refrigerate until ready to use.

2 *Spinach Salad with Crispy Tofu:* Press tofu slices as direct in Tip, right. Once pressed, cut into ½-inch (1 cm) cubes. In a bowl, combine soy sauce, sesame oil, rice wine vinegar and chili sauce. Add tofu cubes and marinate for 20 to 30 minutes, turning the tofu so it gets submerged all over in marinade.

3 Place tofu cubes on two cooking trays. Spray with cooking spray.

4 Place a drip pan in the bottom of the cooking chamber. Place drip pan in the bottom of the cooking chamber. Using the display panel, select **AIR FRY**, adjust **TEMPERATURE** to 400°F (200°C) and set **TIME** for 20 minutes then select **START. PREHEAT** Vortex until display indicates **ADD FOOD**.

5 Slide trays into the middle and bottom positions. Turn tofu after 7 minutes and again after 14-minutes, cooking until browned and crisp.

6 In a large bowl, combine spinach, grated carrot, cucumber, bell pepper and red onion; drizzle with a little dressing and toss to combine. Transfer to serving platter or individual plates. Top with crispy tofu, sprinkle with sesame seeds and drizzle with dressing.

1 tbsp (15 mL) chili sauce (such as sambal oelek)

Olive oil or coconut oil cooking spray

6 cups (1.5 L) baby spinach

1 carrot, grated

½ English cucumber, halved and sliced

½ red bell pepper, thinly sliced

¼ red onion, thinly sliced

3 tbsp (45 mL) sesame seeds, toasted

TIPS It's important to drain the tofu, so here is my quick method. Slice tofu into eight ½-inch (1 cm) thick slices and lay them on a clean folded tea towel. Top with a second folded tea towel and add pressure on top to draw out excess moisture. The easiest way to add pressure is to place something like a wooden cutting board on the tea towel and then weight it down with heavy things, such as tin cans, a cast-iron pan or cookbooks. Leave it for 30 minutes.

ZUCCHINI FRITTERS
WITH ROASTED TOMATOES

MAKES 4 SERVINGS

DF

These fritters are unbelievably easy to make and the perfect way to sneak in some veggies.

PREP TIME
15 minutes

COOK TIME
12 minutes

VORTEX PROGRAMS
▶ Roast
▶ Air Fry

ROASTED TOMATOES

2 cups (500 mL) grape tomatoes

Olive oil cooking spray

Salt and freshly ground black pepper

ZUCCHINI FRITTERS

2 medium zucchini

1 tbsp (15 mL) salt

1 egg, lightly beaten

¼ cup (60 mL) all-purpose or gluten-free all-purpose flour

¼ cup (60 mL) grated Parmesan cheese

continued →

1 *Roasted Tomatoes:* Place tomatoes on a cooking tray; spritz all over with cooking spray and season with salt and pepper.

2 Place drip pan in the bottom of the cooking chamber. Using the display panel, select **ROAST**, adjust **TEMPERATURE** to 350°F (180°C) and set **TIME** to 7 minutes. Press **START**. **PREHEAT** Vortex until display indicates **ADD FOOD**.

3 Slide cooking tray into middle position. When display indicates **TURN FOOD**, stir tomatoes. Cook until lightly browned and skins are beginning to pop. Transfer to a bowl and let cool to room temperature.

4 *Zucchini Fritters:* Using the large grate on a box grater, grate the zucchini. Place in a large bowl, add salt and toss to combine. Let zucchini rest for 10 minutes, then place in a paper towel or tea towel and squeeze as much of the moisture out as possible until it is dry.

5 Place back in bowl and add egg, flour, cheese, herbs, green onions, garlic powder, onion powder, salt, paprika and pepper; stir with a fork just until moistened.

6 Using the display panel, select **AIR FRY**, adjust **TEMPERATURE** to 400°F (200°C) and set **TIME** to 14 minutes. Press **START**. **PREHEAT** Vortex until display indicates **ADD FOOD**.

7 Using the drip pan, drop 4 heaping tablespoons (15 mL each) of batter onto the pan. Lightly spritz with cooking spray. Slide cooking tray into middle position. When display indicates **TURN FOOD**, flip fritters over. Cook until lightly browned. Transfer to a plate and keep warm. Repeat with remaining batter.

1 tbsp (15 mL) chopped fresh herbs, such as parsley, thyme and oregano (or 1 tsp/5 mL dried)

2 tbsp (30 mL) chopped green onions

1 tsp (5 mL) garlic powder

1 tsp (5 mL) onion powder

½ tsp (2 mL) salt

¼ tsp (1 mL) paprika

¼ tsp (1 mL) freshly ground black pepper

Olive oil cooking spray

Sour cream or yogurt (optional)

8 To serve, top fritters with Roasted Tomatoes and a side of sour cream, if using.

TIP It's important to squeeze as much of the liquid out of the zucchini first before adding to the recipe to make sure you don't have a soggy middle in the fritter. Place grated zucchini in a dish cloth or tea towel and pull up into a ball. Squeeze out excess water until dry, then add to recipe.

"THESE FRITTERS ARE UNBELIEVABLY EASY TO MAKE AND THE PERFECT WAY TO SNEAK IN SOME VEGGIES."

SIDES

CHARRED SESAME SHISHITO PEPPERS

MAKES 4 SERVINGS

I recently discovered these addictive little nibblers on the appetizer menu at a local restaurant. When I found them in bags in the grocery store I was excited to try cooking them in the Vortex. Shishito peppers are slim green mild peppers hiding a flavorful secret — one in ten packs a burst of heat. While they are tasty raw, blistering them makes them taste even better.

PREP TIME
5 minutes

COOK TIME
8 minutes

VORTEX PROGRAM
▶ Roast

1 tbsp (15 mL) soy sauce or tamari

2 tsp (10 mL) hot sauce, such as Sriracha

4 tsp (20 mL) sesame oil, divided

1 package (8 oz/227 g) shishito peppers, washed and dried

Toasted sesame seeds

Salt

1 In a small bowl, combine soy sauce, hot sauce and 3 tsp (15 mL) of sesame oil; mix well and set aside.

2 In a medium-size bowl, drizzle shishito peppers with remaining 1 tsp (5 mL) of sesame oil; toss to coat. Lay peppers out on single cooking tray.

3 Place drip pan in the bottom of cooking chamber. Using the display panel, select **ROAST**, adjust **TEMPERATURE** to 375°F (190°C) and set **TIME** to 5 minutes. **PREHEAT** Vortex until display indicates **ADD FOOD**.

4 Place cooking tray in middle position. When display indicates **TURN FOOD**, toss peppers gently. Cook until lightly charred and tender.

5 Transfer to a serving dish, add reserved hot sauce mixture and garnish with toasted sesame seeds and a sprinkling of salt.

VARIATION *Lime Cilantro Shishito Peppers:* Toss peppers in 1 tbsp (15 mL) olive oil and cook as above. When cooked, removed from the oven, add juice of 1 lime, 2 tbsp (30 mL) chopped fresh cilantro and 1 tsp (5 mL) flaky coarse finishing salt, such as Maldon salt; toss to combine. Serve warm.

CHEDDAR, CHIVE & GARLIC BISCUITS

MAKES 9 SERVINGS

These biscuits are over-the-top wonderful. They are perfect to serve with a soup or stew. When you break into the freshly baked biscuit, you'll see warm, melty cheese and you just know they are going to taste good.

PREP TIME
15 minutes

COOK TIME
12 minutes

VORTEX PROGRAM
▶ Bake

---

2 tbsp (30 mL) butter, softened

1 tsp (5 mL) minced garlic

2 cups (500 mL) all-purpose flour

1 tbsp (15 mL) baking powder

½ tsp (2 mL) salt

2 cups (500 mL) grated sharp (old) Cheddar cheese

3 tbsp (45 mL) chopped fresh chives

1 cup + 3 tbsp (250 mL + 45 mL) whipping cream

Olive oil cooking spray

1 In a small bowl, mix together butter and garlic; set aside.

2 In a large bowl, whisk together flour, baking powder and salt. Stir in cheese and chives. Add cream and stir with a stiff spatula just until a shaggy dough forms, about 30 seconds. Turn dough out onto a lightly floured surface and press into a 6-inch (15 cm) square.

3 Using a very sharp knife or dough scraper, cut dough into nine square biscuits. Place biscuits on drip tray, positioning them around the outside edge of the tray. Spray lightly with cooking spray.

4 Using the display panel, select **BAKE**, adjust **TEMPERATURE** to 400°F (200°C) and set **TIME** to 12 minutes. **PREHEAT** Vortex until display indicates **ADD FOOD**.

5 Slide drip tray into middle position and bake until biscuits are golden and puffed, rotating pan halfway through baking. Let cool 5 minutes before transferring to a wire rack. Spread garlic butter over tops of biscuits. Serve warm.

TIPS I prefer to bake these biscuits one tray at a time. Transfer baked biscuits to a cooling rack; then you can repeat baking with remaining dough. However, you will need to reset the machine.

These biscuits are a very generous size. Feel free to cut them smaller and make a few more.

I like to make these with sharp (old) Cheddar, but they are also quite delicious made with Swiss or Gouda cheese.

CHILI CHEESE ROASTED WHOLE CAULIFLOWER

MAKES 4 TO 6 SERVINGS

If you have never had a whole roasted cauliflower, you are missing out. The Vortex creates a crusty coating that tastes amazing.

PREP TIME
5 minutes

COOK TIME
20 minutes

VORTEX PROGRAM
▶ Air Fry

1 whole medium cauliflower, trimmed

1/2 cup (125 mL) sour cream (14%)

1/3 cup (75 mL) finely grated Parmesan cheese

1 tsp (5 mL) salt

1/2 tsp (2 mL) chili powder

1/4 tsp (1 mL) freshly ground black pepper

1 Remove all the leaves from the head of the cauliflower and cut out the stem, while keeping the head of the whole cauliflower intact as much as possible.

2 In a small bowl, mix the sour cream, cheese, salt, chili powder and pepper. Place cauliflower on cooking tray and spread sour cream mixture over the entire surface of the cauliflower. Place cooking tray into the middle position in the cooking chamber. Set drip tray in the bottom of the cooking chamber.

3 Set Vortex to **AIR FRY**, adjust **TEMPERATURE** to 360°F (182°C) and set **TIME** to 20 minutes. (The cauliflower will cook through the preheating time as well.) Cook until cauliflower is browned on top and tender crisp. Serve whole.

TIPS Cooked in the Vortex, the cauliflower will not be as tender all the way through as compared to when cooked in the oven. But the outer part is tender and the flavor is delicious, plus it's crispier.

When buying cauliflower heads, look for heavy, firm and compact heads without any brown spotting. The florets should be very tight together and any leaves should be tightly wrapped around the florets.

To prepare the cauliflower for roasting, remove the leaves and cut as much of the stem out of the cauliflower as you can so that it lies flat on the cooking tray.

MARINATED BRUSSELS SPROUTS
WITH BACON

MAKES 4 TO 6 SERVINGS

This recipe is courtesy of my sister Glenda. She and her daughter have brought this dish to many a family gathering, so when I told her I wanted to try it in my Vortex, she gladly shared. Vegans can skip the bacon — it has lots of flavor from the garlicky marinade anyhow.

PREP TIME
15 minutes

COOK TIME
8 minutes

VORTEX PROGRAMS
▶ **Roast**
▶ **Rotate**

1 lb (500 g) Brussels sprouts, ends trimmed and cut in half

4 slices prosciutto, bacon or pancetta, cut into wide slices

3 tbsp (45 mL) olive oil

3 cloves garlic, sliced

1 tsp (5 mL) salt

½ tsp (2 mL) freshly ground black pepper

1 tbsp (15 mL) balsamic glaze (optional)

▶ ROTISSERIE BASKET AND LIFT
▶ SEALABLE BAG

1 In a sealable bag, place halved Brussels sprouts, prosciutto slices, olive oil, garlic, salt and pepper. Seal bag, then massage all ingredients together. Marinate 4 to 6 hours or refrigerate overnight.

2 Transfer Brussels sprouts to the rotisserie basket and secure lid in place. Using the rotisserie lift, lift the basket into the oven and slide the basket spit along the side bars until spit reaches the rotisserie hole. Pull forward on the red release lever to secure the ends of the basket spit in place.

3 Place the drip pan in the bottom of the cooking chamber. Close door. Using the display panel, select **ROAST** and **ROTATE**, adjust **TEMPERATURE** to 380°F (193°C) and set **TIME** to 8 minutes. Press **START** and ignore **ADD FOOD** message. Cook until vegetables are tender and prosciutto is cooked inside.

4 When unit finishes cooking, use rotisserie lift to remove basket, pulling forward on the red release lever to remove basket spit. Use oven mitts to remove lid. Serve hot and drizzled with balsamic glaze, if desired.

TIP These Brussels sprouts are also delicious cold, as a salad. You can serve with pomegranate seeds, toasted walnuts and crumbled goat's cheese. Feel free to add another tablespoon (15 mL) of olive oil before serving.

MEXICAN STREET CORN SALAD

MAKES 4 SERVINGS

GF

In Mexico, cobs of corn garnished with spices and cheese are street fare. This version puts it all in a salad, is a much less messy way to eat it and is super creamy with tons of flavor. It's perfect in summer when corn is in season, but easy to do with frozen corn any time of the year. Serve alongside tacos!

PREP TIME
10 minutes

COOK TIME
15 minutes

VORTEX PROGRAM
▶ **Roast**

ROASTED CORN

3 tbsp (45 mL) melted butter or olive oil

1 tsp (5 mL) ground cumin

1 tsp (5 mL) garlic powder

½ tsp (2 mL) salt

¼ tsp (1 mL) red pepper flakes

4 cobs fresh corn, husked and silk removed, or 2 cups (500 mL) frozen corn, thawed

DRESSING

2 tbsp (30 mL) mayonnaise

1 green onion, finely sliced

½ tsp (2 mL) chili powder

½ tsp (2 mL) garlic powder

Zest and juice of 1 lime

Salt

1 tbsp (15 mL) chopped fresh cilantro or parsley

½ cup (125 mL) cojita or feta cheese, crumbled

▶ SEALABLE BAG

1 *Roasted Corn:* In a bowl, mix together melted butter, cumin, garlic powder, salt and red pepper flakes. Pour into a sealable bag and add cobs of corn. Seal the bag and massage the paste all over the corn. Transfer onto cooking tray (or drip pan if using thawed corn niblets.)

2 Using the display panel, select **AIR FRY**, adjust **TEMPERATURE** to 400°F (200°C) and set **TIME** to 15 minutes. **PREHEAT** Vortex until display indicates **ADD FOOD**.

3 Place cooking tray in middle position. When display indicates **TURN FOOD**, turn corn cobs over (or stir corn niblets). Cook until lightly charred and tender. Remove from oven and allow to cool; then, using a sharp knife, cut corn off cobs.

4 *Dressing:* Meanwhile, in a medium bowl, combine mayonnaise, green onion, chili and garlic powder, lime zest, lime juice and salt to taste. Stir corn into dressing along with cilantro and cheese, if using; mix well to combine. Chill until ready to serve. Garnish with more cheese and cilantro or parsley if you wish.

VARIATION To make vegan version of this salad, use vegan mayonnaise and a vegan feta substitute in place of the regular mayonnaise and cojita cheese.

PARMESAN SPAGHETTI SQUASH

MAKES 4 TO 6 SERVINGS

GF

I have been making squash with Parmesan for years. It was an easy way to get my children to eat their veggies when they were young. One of my favorites is spaghetti squash. I love how the strands just pull apart like noodles and I can top it with a favorite sauce or just enjoy it on its own.

PREP TIME
5 minutes

COOK TIME
40 minutes

VORTEX PROGRAM
▶ **Roast**

---

1 spaghetti squash, about 1½ to 2 lbs (750 g to 1 kg), halved and seeded

Olive oil cooking spray

Salt and freshly ground black pepper

2 tbsp (30 mL) butter

2 cloves garlic, minced

2 tbsp (30 mL) freshly grated Parmesan cheese

1 tbsp (15 mL) chopped fresh parsley (optional)

1 Spray prepared spaghetti squash with cooking spray on all sides. Season cut sides with salt and pepper then place cut sides down on cooking tray.

2 Place drip pan in the bottom of cooking chamber. Using the display panel, select **ROAST**, adjust **TEMPERATURE** to 360°F (182°C) and set **TIME** to 40 minutes. Press **START**. **PREHEAT** Vortex until display indicates **ADD FOOD**.

3 Cook until inside of squash is very tender and shreds easily when raked with a fork. (It should almost be the consistency of al dente pasta.) Cool slightly, then shred as much of the flesh as possible and transfer to a large bowl. Discard the outside skin.

4 In a large skillet, melt butter over medium heat. Add garlic and cook 30 seconds just until fragrant. Add squash and sauté over medium heat, stirring occasionally for 5 minutes until heated through. Add cheese and parsley and stir just until combined. Serve immediately.

TIP To cut a spaghetti squash in half, cut a small slice off the bottom with a heavy knife and stand the squash upright. Plunge the tip of the knife into the squash near the stem end and cut straight down to the bottom. Repeat on the other side from stem to bottom and split the squash in half. Use a paring knife to cut out the seeds and a spoon to scrape it out.

PESTO PANKO GREEN BEANS

MAKES 4 SERVINGS

These green beans are a quick and fun way to up a side dish. Aromatic basil pesto, either store-bought or homemade, stores well in your fridge and adds a delicious flavor boost to the beans. I like them as a side dish to fish or pork but they make a fun appetizer too.

PREP TIME
5 minutes

COOK TIME
10 minutes

VORTEX PROGRAM
▶ **Air Fry**

---

1 lb (500 g) green beans, end trimmed, but left whole

¼ cup (60 mL) prepared basil pesto, store-bought or homemade

½ cup (125 mL) grated Parmesan cheese

⅓ cup (75 mL) panko bread crumbs

½ tsp (2 mL) salt

¼ tsp (1 mL) freshly ground black pepper

Olive oil cooking spray

1 In a large bowl, combine green beans and pesto. Using your hands, toss the beans with the pesto so they are evenly coated.

2 In a separate bowl, combine cheese, panko, salt and pepper; stir to combine and pour over beans. Toss again to coat and place beans on one cooking tray. Lightly spray beans with cooking spray.

3 Place drip pan in the bottom of cooking chamber. Using the display panel, select **AIR FRY**, adjust **TEMPERATURE** to 375°F (190°C) and set **TIME** to 10 minutes. **PREHEAT** Vortex until display indicates **ADD FOOD**.

4 Place cooking tray in middle position. When display indicates **TURN FOOD**, toss very gently so as to not lose too much of the panko coating. Cook until lightly golden and crisp. Serve warm.

TIPS You can easily make this a gluten-free dish by using gluten-free panko bread crumbs. You can also use regular gluten-free bread crumbs if you can't find the panko style.

ROASTED CORN CORNBREAD

MAKES 6 TO 8 SERVINGS

There is nothing better to serve alongside a pot of chili than a warm chunk of cornbread. While some purists would say it should be plain and simple, I have filled mine with roasted sweet corn and peppers. It's best made when corn is fresh and in season, but delicious using frozen corn too.

PREP TIME
20 minutes

COOK TIME
10 minutes + 25 minutes

VORTEX PROGRAMS
▶ Roast
▶ Bake

1 onion, diced

½ red bell pepper, seeded and diced

1 small jalapeño pepper, minced

1 cup (250 mL) fresh or frozen corn, thawed if frozen

1 tbsp (15 mL) olive oil

1 tbsp (15 mL) brown sugar

½ cup (125 mL) vegetable oil

3 eggs

½ cup (125 mL) cornmeal

½ cup (125 mL) regular or gluten-free all-purpose flour

2 tsp (10 mL) baking powder

½ tsp (2 mL) salt

½ tsp (2 mL) freshly ground black pepper

½ cup (125 mL) grated sharp (old) Cheddar cheese

½ cup (125 mL) chopped fresh cilantro or parsley

▶ 8- BY 8-INCH (20 BY 20 CM) SQUARE OR 8-INCH (20 CM) ROUND BAKING PAN

1 Place onion, bell pepper, jalapeño pepper and corn in baking pan. Drizzle with 1 tbsp (15 mL) olive oil and sprinkle with brown sugar; toss to combine.

2 Turn drip tray upside down and place in the bottom position. Using the display panel, select ROAST, adjust TEMPERATURE to 380°F (193°C) and set TIME to 10 minutes. Press START. PREHEAT Vortex until display indicates ADD FOOD. When display indicates TURN FOOD, give vegetables a stir and continue cooking until slightly golden and beginning to brown. Remove from cooking chamber to cool.

3 Meanwhile, in a bowl, whisk together vegetable oil and eggs until well combined. In a separate bowl, whisk together cornmeal, flour, baking powder, salt and pepper. Add flour mixture to egg mixture along with cheese, cilantro and roasted vegetables, folding ingredients together just until mixed. Spread the batter into the baking pan.

4 Using the display panel, select BAKE, adjust TEMPERATURE to 325°F (160°C) and set TIME to 25 minutes. Press START. PREHEAT Vortex until display indicates ADD FOOD. Place baking tray on drip pan and bake until golden and toothpick comes out clean when inserted in the center. Serve warm with Jalapeño Butter (see Tip).

TO make Jalapeño Butter: In a bowl, combine ¼ cup (60 mL) softened butter with ¼ cup (60 mL) jalapeño jelly.

If you use a gluten-free all-purpose flour, the resulting cornbread will be equally as delicious but just a little more crumbly.

THE BEST FRIES

MAKES 4 SERVINGS

I can't imagine writing a cookbook about an appliance that air fries without including a recipe for french fries. The Vortex works some kind of magic on potatoes. The key is soaking the fries in cold water to remove some of their starch content. This also helps the centers get tender and the outsides get crispy. Because you are not frying them in a lot of oil, go ahead and dip them into a decadent Smoked Paprika Aïoli, but some good old-fashioned ketchup is always a winner too!

PREP TIME
10 minutes

CHILLING TIME
30 minutes or up to
24 hours

COOK TIME
20 minutes

VORTEX PROGRAM
▶ **Air Fry**
▶ **Rotate**

1 lb (500 g) russet potatoes, scrubbed

2 tsp (10 mL) olive oil

1 tbsp (15 mL) chili powder

1 tsp (5 mL) ground cumin

1 tsp (5 mL) kosher salt

Freshly ground black pepper

▶ ROTISSERIE BASKET AND LIFT

1 Cut potatoes into ¼ inch (0.5 cm) slices, about 2 to 3 inches (5 to 7.5 cm) long. Place in a large bowl, cover with water and chill 30 minutes or up to 24 hours.

2 Drain potatoes and pat dry with a tea towel. Place back in bowl and toss with oil, chili powder, cumin, salt and pepper; toss well to coat. Transfer to rotisserie basket and secure lid.

3 Place the drip pan in the bottom of the cooking chamber. Using the rotisserie lift attachment, lift the rotisserie basket into the cooking chamber and slide along the side bars until spit reaches the rotisserie hole. Pull forward on the red release lever to secure the ends of the spit in place, then close door. Using the display panel, select **AIR FRY** and **ROTATE**, adjust **TEMPERATURE** to 400°F (200°C) and select **TIME** to 20 minutes. Select **START**.

4 Fries are cooked when golden and tender. Serve hot.

TIPS It's important not to overcrowd the rotisserie basket. If you overload the basket, you may end up create a steaming effect instead of a crisping effect.

Feel free to switch up your spices. You can substitute smoked paprika for the chili powder and garlic powder or onion powder for the ground cumin.

VARIATION *Sweet Potato Fries:* Prepare fries the same way using sweet potatoes. You can leave them plain by just adding salt, or season with the 1 tsp (5 mL) sweet or hot smoked paprika.

SMOKED PAPRIKA AÏOLI
MAKES $1/_2$ CUP (125 ML)

This aïoli is excellent with regular or sweet potato fries

½ cup (125 mL) mayonnaise

2 cloves garlic, minced

½ tsp (2 mL) lemon juice

½ tsp (2 mL) smoked paprika

1 In a bowl, combine mayonnaise, garlic, lemon juice and smoked paprika. Mix well and allow to sit 10 minutes before serving for flavors to meld.

SNACKS

PEPPERED BEEF JERKY

MAKES 2 TO 4 SERVINGS

My son Jack is a huge fan of beef jerky, so we decided to give it a try. There is a little extra work because you need to freeze the meat first, then marinate it. But the dehydrator function easily turns it into a delicious snack. It's full of savory flavors, includes no added sweeteners and is irresistibly delicious.

FREEZING TIME
1 to 2 hours

PREP TIME
10 minutes

MARINATING TIME
3 hours to overnight

COOK TIME
3 to 3½ hours

VORTEX PROGRAM
▶ Dehydrate

1 lb (500 g) flank steak

½ cup (125 mL) soy sauce

2 tbsp (30 mL) Worcestershire sauce

2 tsp (10 mL) coarsely cracked black pepper

1 tsp (5 mL) onion powder

1 tsp (5 mL) seasoned salt

½ tsp (2 mL) garlic powder

▶ SEALABLE FREEZER BAG

1 Place flank steak in a sealable freezer bag and freeze for 1 to 2 hours to firm the meat for slicing.

2 Slice steak against the grain into ⅛- to ¼-inch (3 mm to 0.5 cm) thick strips.

3 In a glass bowl, combine soy sauce, Worcestershire sauce, pepper, onion powder, seasoned salt and garlic powder. Add beef strips and mix to ensure strips are coated on all sides with marinade. Refrigerate covered 3 to 4 hours or overnight.

4 Remove meat and pat dry. Divide steak strips between the two cooking trays, in an even layer, making sure strips don't overlap.

5 Place drip pan in the bottom of the cooking chamber and insert one cooking tray in the top position and one in the middle position.

6 Using the display panel, select **DEHYDRATE**, adjust **TEMPERATURE** to 160°F (70°C) and set **TIME** for 3 hours, then touch **START**.

7 After 1½ hours, switch the cooking trays so that the tray in the top position moves to the middle and the tray in the middle moves to the top position.

8 When the dehydrator program is nearly complete, test a piece of jerky by bending it at a 90-degree angle. If any moisture seeps out, return for an additional 20 to 30 minutes of cooking time. If it bends but there is no moisture seepage, it is done. If it cracks and breaks, it is overdone.

TIPS Use lean cuts of beef for making jerky. I really like flank steak, but eye of round or top or bottom round are also good options and a little more economical.

Slice the beef as thin as possible. For tender jerky, slice meat against the grain; for chewier, slice with the grain. Freezing steak for a few hours allows you to slice it very thinly.

BACON CANDY

MAKES 12 STRIPS, 4 TO 6 SERVINGS

Making candied bacon was one of those aha moments — in other words, why didn't I do this before? The magic all happens in the Vortex and it takes only half an hour. Eat it as it is, crumble into salads or use it to garnish my Crispy Deviled Eggs (page 35).

PREP TIME
5 minutes

COOK TIME
15 minutes

VORTEX PROGRAM
▶ Air Fry

¼ cup (60 mL) light brown sugar

¼ tsp (1 mL) smoked paprika

8 strips bacon, not thick cut

1 tsp (5 mL) freshly cracked black pepper

1 In a bowl, combine brown sugar and smoked paprika.

2 Lay bacon strips on two cooking trays. Grind pepper onto slices, and then sprinkle with half of the brown sugar mixture.

3 Place a drip pan in the bottom of the cooking chamber. Using the display panel, select **AIR FRY** then adjust **TEMPERATURE** to 350°F (180°C) and set **TIME** to 10 minutes then press **START**. **PREHEAT** Vortex until display indicates **ADD FOOD**.

4 Set cooking trays into top and middle positions. When display indicates **TURN FOOD**, turn bacon slices over and sprinkle with remaining brown sugar. Switch trays so that the tray in the middle position moves to the bottom and the tray in the bottom moves to the top. Cook until bacon is crunchy, ensuring it doesn't burn. Remove from cooking chamber and set aside to cool for 5 minutes. Bacon will crisp as it cools.

TIPS Bacon can be stored in the fridge for a few days and reheats well in Vortex.

Use in any sandwich from grilled cheese to a chicken or turkey club.

One of my favorite ways to use candied bacon is to crumble a little on vanilla ice cream.

FO' CHEEZY KALE CHIPS

MAKES 2 SERVINGS

If you are a fan of kale chips, you'll love these nacho-like crisps! They satisfy every chip craving — cheesy, salty and crispy! You need the slow drying process of the dehydrate function to get them good and crunchy.

PREP TIME
20 minutes

COOK TIME
4 hours

VORTEX PROGRAM
▶ **Dehydrate**

---

1 cup (250 mL) raw cashews

¼ cup (60 mL) chopped oil-packed sun-dried tomatoes

2 cloves garlic

¾ cup (175 mL) water

2 tsp (10 mL) dried basil

2 tbsp (30 mL) lemon juice

2 tbsp (30 mL) nutritional yeast

½ tsp (2 mL) salt, or to taste

1 bunch curly kale, washed and dried

▶ FOOD PROCESSOR

1 Place cashews in a bowl and cover with water. Let stand for at least 1 hour until softened. Drain and place in a food processor.

2 Add tomatoes, garlic, water, basil, lemon juice, nutritional yeast and salt. Process until smooth. Taste and adjust seasoning.

3 Remove stems from kale leaves, discarding the stems. Tear leaves into smaller "chip" size pieces. Place in a large bowl. Pour the sauce over the kale leaves, then massage the sauce into the kale using your hands until all the kale is well coated. Lay leaves out onto the drip pan and cooking trays and season with a little more salt. (You will probably need to do this in two batches, so put remaining kale in a sealable container and refrigerate up to 24 hours.)

4 Slide trays into bottom, middle and top positions. Using the display panel, select **DEHYDRATE**, adjust **TEMPERATURE** to 110°F (43°C) and set **TIME** to 4 hours. Press **START**. **DEHYDRATE** until kale chips dried. Repeat with any remaining kale leaves.

TIPS Don't confuse nutritional yeast with quick-rising or traditional yeast — they are not the same thing. Nutritional yeast is specifically used as a food. The yeast cells are killed during manufacturing and are not alive in the final product. The yeast has a flaky texture and a cheesy, nutty flavor. It is naturally low in sodium and calories as well as fat-, sugar- and gluten-free.

HOMEMADE TORTILLA CHIPS
WITH FRESH PICO DE GALLO

MAKES 2 TO 4 SERVINGS

This might be a dangerous thing since you can get perfectly fresh and crunchy tortilla chips made with the Vortex rotisserie basket. Paired with this Fresh Pico de Gallo, it makes a great light snack.

PREP TIME

5 minutes

COOK TIME

8 minutes

VORTEX PROGRAM

▸ **Air Fry**

▸ **Rotate**

HOMEMADE TORTILLA CHIPS

8 fresh corn tortillas

Nonstick cooking spray

Salt

FRESH PICO DE GALLO

3 plum tomatoes, seeded and diced

2 sprigs fresh cilantro, chopped

1 small jalapeño pepper, seeded and finely chopped

½ small red onion, finely chopped

1 clove garlic, grated or minced

Dash hot sauce

Juice of 1 lime

Salt

▸ ROTISSERIE BASKET

▸ ROTISSERIE LIFT

1 *Homemade Tortilla Chips:* Lightly spray corn tortillas with cooking spray. Cut each tortilla into eight wedges. Season liberally with salt and toss to coat.

2 Load tortilla wedges into rotisserie basket and secure lid in place. Place the drip pan in the bottom of the cooking chamber. Using the rotisserie lift tool, slide the rotisserie basket along the side bars until it reaches the rotisserie hole. Pull forward to the red release lever to secure the ends of the basket in place. Close door.

3 Using the display panel, select **AIR FRY** and **ROTATE**, adjust **TEMPERATURE** to 400°F (200°C) and set **TIME** to 8 minutes. Press START.

4 Remove basket from cooking chamber by pulling forward on the red release lever and lifting out using the rotisserie lift tool. Allow basket to cool for 5 minutes before removing lid. Transfer to serving bowl and serve with Fresh Pico de Gallo.

5 *Fresh Pico de Gallo:* In a bowl, combine tomatoes, cilantro, jalapeño, red onion, garlic, hot sauce and lime juice; stir to combine. Season to taste with salt.

TIPS Look for fresh corn tortillas in the refrigerated section of the grocery store or in a Latin grocery store.

I first spray the tortillas with oil, and then cut them into wedges. It makes for fast, efficient work.

SNACKING POTATO CHIPS

MAKES 2 TO 4 SERVINGS

Most people would say they are either a sweet or savory fan. Personally I like sweet, but I can be convinced to eat a potato chip now and again if they are not too greasy. These ones were killer for me! They take a little work not to burn them, but the effort is totally worth it.

PREP TIME
5 minutes

COOK TIME
15 minutes

VORTEX PROGRAM
▶ **Air Fry**

---

1 lb (500 g) russet potatoes, washed and dried

1 tbsp (15 mL) olive oil

1 tsp (15 mL) salt

▶ MANDOLIN

1 Using a mandoline or very sharp knife, slice potatoes into even ⅛-inch (3 mm) slices.

2 In a large bowl, toss with olive oil and salt, making sure potato slices are all well coated with oil. Place 9 to 12 slices on cooking tray at one time, so that they don't overlap.

3 Place drip pan in the bottom of cooking chamber. Select **AIR FRY**, adjust **TEMPERATURE** to 370°F (188°C) and set **TIME** to 3 minutes. **PREHEAT** Vortex until display indicates **ADD FOOD**.

4 Place cooking trays in bottom and middle positions. Cook in 3-minute increments, each time removing trays and turning potato slices over then resetting **TIME** for 3 minutes and switching trays positions so that bottom tray moves to the middle position and middle tray moves to the bottom and then back again. Do not flip potatoes when display indicates **TURN FOOD**. Just let them continue to cook. This will take about three to four rounds of 3 minutes each to achieve the perfect crisp, switching tray position and turning potatoes over until golden and crisp. Allow potatoes to cool completely before eating.

TIP Using a mandoline slicer with a guard is the best way to get perfect consistent slices on the potato. Set the thickness of slice to ⅛-inch (3 mm). If you don't have a mandoline slicer, a sharp knife is your next best option.

PEANUT BUTTER BANANA CHIPS

MAKES 2 TO 4 SERVINGS

The bonus of the Vortex machine is that it can also make delicious snacks like these banana chips. Dusted in peanut butter powder (available in health food stores), these are an addictive, gluten-free, vegan snack. They also make a great addition to a homemade protein bar — a quick three-ingredient mixture that's easy to blend up if you have a food processor or blender.

PREP TIME
10 minutes

COOK TIME
8 hours

VORTEX PROGRAM
▶ Dehydrate

2 ripe bananas
2 tbsp (30 mL) peanut butter powder

1 Slice the bananas into thin (¼-inch/0.5 cm) slices and arrange them in a single layer on two baking sheets.

2 Sprinkle with peanut butter powder on one side, then flip slices over and sprinkle the second side.

3 Place the drip pan in the bottom of the cooking chamber. Using the display panel, select DEHYDRATE, adjust TEMPERATURE to 135°F (57°C) and set TIME to 8 hours. Insert one cooking tray into the top position and the other tray into the bottom position. Close the door. DEHYDRATE until chips are dried, but not rock hard. Transfer to a cooling rack and cool completely before storing.

4 Store banana chips in an airtight container at room temperature for at least 2 weeks.

TIPS The key to getting a good batch of dehydrated banana chips is to cut the bananas into uniformly thin slices. Aim for ¼-inch (0.5 cm), but if you cut them a little thicker that will work too.

Keep an eye on the banana chips for the last couple of hours so that you can remove them when they reach the texture you want. Ideally you want chewy dehydrated banana chips.

HOMEMADE PROTEIN BARS
MAKES 6 BARS

Use your Peanut Butter Banana Chips to make your own portable power bars.

1 cup (250 mL) dehydrated Peanut Butter Banana Chips

½ cup (125 mL) medjool dates, pitted and chopped

⅔ cup (150 mL) walnuts

▸ FOOD PROCESSOR OR BLENDER
▸ 8- BY 4-INCH (20 BY 10 CM) LOAF PAN

1 Place banana chips, dates and walnuts in a food processor. Pulse 1 to 2 minutes until everything is uniformly finely chopped but not a paste. Transfer to an 8- by 4-inch (20 by 10 cm) loaf pan and press down to make it level. Refrigerate for 1 hour, then cut into six bars. Transfer bars to an airtight container and refrigerate.

TAPAS TOMATO CHIPS

MAKES 1 CUP

There is nothing like fresh garden tomatoes. But if you have a garden full of prolific plants, these snacking chips are just the answer to finding another way to use them. I added them to a charcuterie board and they were the perfect salty crunch with a selection of cheeses, meats and condiments.

PREP TIME
10 minutes

COOK TIME
8 to 10 hours

VORTEX PROGRAM
▶ **Dehydrate**

---

4 large plum (Roma) tomatoes, sliced ¼-inch (0.5 cm) thick

½ tsp (2 mL) dried basil or herbes de Provence

Kosher salt

1 Place sliced tomatoes on two cooking trays. Sprinkle very lightly with salt and basil, but on one side only.

2 Place drip pan in bottom of cooking chamber. Place cooking trays in top and middle positions. Close door. Using the display panel, select **DEHYDRATE**, adjust **TEMPERATURE** to 135°F (57°C) and set **TIME** to 8 or 10 hours (depending on how thick you cut the tomatoes). Press **START**.

3 **DEHYDRATE** until almost crispy, but make sure they are not over dry. You want them to be slightly pliable.

VARIATION Homemade Air-Dried Tomatoes in Oil: If you decide to make a few batches of these tomato chips, you can preserve them in oil and use them in recipes that call for sundried tomatoes. Layer tomato chips in a clean jar with a few fresh basil leaves, half a fresh rosemary sprig, a pinch more salt, freshly ground black pepper, dried basil and oregano. Cover in olive oil and store in the refrigerator.

STRAWBERRIES & CREAM FRUIT LEATHER

MAKES 1 PAN

This unique fruit leather is made with pureed strawberries, applesauce and yogurt — so few ingredients for such a great result. The dehydrator function makes this fun. The result is a tangy and sweet strawberry and vanilla fruit leather that you will never find in any grocery store.

PREP TIME
5 minutes

COOK TIME
12 hours

VORTEX FUNCTION
▶ Dehydrator

¼ cup (60 mL) puréed strawberries

¼ cup (60 mL) unsweetened applesauce

1 cup (250 mL) plain full-fat yogurt

1 tsp (5 mL) vanilla

1 In a bowl, combine orange juice concentrate, applesauce, yogurt and vanilla. Mix well and pour onto drip pan, spreading evenly with a spatula.

2 Using the display panel, select **DEHYDRATE**, adjust **TEMPERATURE** to 135°F (57°C) and set **TIME** to 12 hours. Slide tray into middle position. Press **START**.

3 When finished, fruit leather should be soft but not tacky or sticky. Allow tray to cool completely.

4 Cut with scissors into strips and store in a sealable bag or an airtight container for up to 1 month.

TIPS Avoid using Greek yogurt for this fruit leather, as it much thicker in consistency and more difficult to dehydrate. Regular full-fat (6%) yogurt is a better option. Have fun with some flavors such as peach or coconut.

For an added twist, I added a ½ tsp (2 mL) balsamic vinegar to the yogurt mixture. There was some cracking in the leather, but I was still able to roll it up.

SPICY MIDDLE EASTERN CHICKPEAS

MAKES ABOUT 1½ CUPS

Roasted chickpeas make a healthy yet addictive snack that is easy to prepare in the Vortex. They become nutty and crunchy once they are baked. Za'atar is a Middle Eastern spice blend of dried thyme, sumac and sesame seeds, but you can use any spice combination you like.

PREP TIME
10 minutes

COOK TIME
15 minutes

VORTEX PROGRAM
▶ Air Fry

---

1 can (19 oz/540 mL) chickpeas, drained and rinsed

1 tbsp (15 mL) za'atar seasoning

2 tsp (10 mL) salt

2 tsp (15 mL) olive oil

⅛ tsp (0.5 mL) cayenne pepper

1 Drain and rinse chickpeas well. Spread out onto a baking sheet and use paper towels to rub over chickpeas to dry. Transfer to a bowl.

2 Stir in za'atar, salt, oil and cayenne pepper; stir to combine. Transfer chickpeas onto two cooking trays.

3 Place the drip pan in the bottom of the cooking chamber. Using display panel, select **AIR FRY**, adjust **TEMPERATURE** to 375°F (190°C) and set **TIME** to 15 minutes, then touch **START**.

4 When Vortex displays **ADD FOOD**, slide cooking trays into the middle and bottom positions.

5 When the display indicates **TURN FOOD**, do not shake pan too much, but switch cooking trays so that the tray in the middle position is in the bottom and the one on the bottom position is in the top.

6 Remove from the cooking chamber when golden brown. Let cool and eat at room temperature.

TIPS Who needs croutons when you have these nibblers? While these crispy chickpeas make a delicious snack, they are the perfect crunch in a salad of crispy chopped romaine, chopped cucumbers, halved cherry tomatoes, chopped parsley and fresh mint. Drizzle salad with a little olive oil and red wine vinegar, plus a sprinkle of salt and pepper.

These crispy chickpeas can be made and stored at room temperature for up to 4 weeks.

DESSERTS

BUTTERSCOTCH BROOKIES

MAKES 24

My millennial friend Linnea Scian suggested we try making a "Brookie" for this cookbook. When I asked her what they were, she told me they are a half cookie, half brownie. I thought this was a fantastic idea because it combines my two favorite desserts.

PREP TIME
20 minutes

COOK TIME
10 minutes

VORTEX PROGRAM
▶ Bake

BROWNIE

½ cup (125 mL) melted butter

¾ cup (175 mL) granulated sugar

½ cup (125 mL) cocoa powder

1 large egg

½ tsp (2 mL) vanilla

1 cup (125 mL) all-purpose flour

½ tsp (2 mL) salt

BUTTERSCOTCH COOKIE

½ cup (125 mL) butter, softened

½ cup (125 mL) packed brown sugar

¼ cup (60 mL) granulated sugar

1 large egg

1 tsp (5 mL) vanilla

1½ cups (375 mL) all-purpose flour

½ tsp (2 mL) baking soda

½ tsp (2 mL) salt

1 cup (250 mL) butterscotch baking chips

Flaky sea salt for sprinkling

1 *Brownie:* In a large bowl with a wooden spoon, combine melted butter, sugar and cocoa powder; mix well. Add egg and vanilla and whisk together until glossy. Add flour and salt and mix, just until combined. Refrigerate while you make the butterscotch cookie dough.

2 *Butterscotch Cookie:* In another large bowl, using wooden spoon, blend together softened butter, brown and white sugars until light and fluffy. Add egg and vanilla and stir until combined. Add flour, baking soda and salt and blend until just combined, then add butterscotch chips and fold in until mixture is completely blended.

3 *To make Butterscotch Brookies:* Using a 1 tbsp (15 mL) measure, scoop out a heaping spoonful of each dough. Roll into balls. Take one brownie ball and one cookie dough ball and roll them together. Repeat with remaining dough. Flatten slightly and sprinkle with sea salt. Place six balls around outside edge of drip pan so the center is empty.

4 Using the display panel, select **BAKE**, adjust **TEMPERATURE** to 325°F (160°C) and set **TIME** to 10 minutes. **PREHEAT** Vortex until display indicates **ADD FOOD**.

5 Slide drip pan tray into middle position and bake until brookies are golden. Let cool 5 minutes before transferring to a wire rack and cool completely.

TIP Since you can only bake six cookies at a time, I like to freeze any uncooked cookies and bake whenever I want a treat. **PREHEAT** Vortex as directed above and bake cookies from frozen for 12 minutes.

CHOCOLATE HAZELNUT PUFF PASTRY DANISH

MAKES 9 TO 12 SERVINGS

One Saturday night I had a craving for something sweet. I happened to have a sheet of thawed puff pastry in my fridge and an open jar of chocolate-hazelnut spread. I got the inspiration for these from my friend who owns the most wonderful neighborhood bakery specializing in French pastries.

PREP TIME
25 minutes

COOK TIME
12 minutes

VORTEX PROGRAMS
▶ Bake

---

1 sheet (½ lb / 250 g) puff pastry, thawed

½ cup (125 mL) chocolate hazelnut spread

1 egg, whisked

Granulated sugar (optional)

1 Unroll puff pastry sheet and cut each sheet into 9 or 12 equal squares, about 3- by 3-inch (7.5 by 7.5 cm) each.

2 Place heaping spoonful (1 tbsp/15 mL) of chocolate hazelnut spread in the center of each square. Brush egg around outside edge of each square. Pinch two opposite ends of each square firmly and flatten the pinched ends. Brush tops of puff pastry with egg, then lay onto cooking trays, about four or five danishes per tray. Place trays in the freezer for 15 minutes to chill.

3 Using display panel, select **BAKE**, adjust **TEMPERATURE** to 360°F (182°C) and set **TIME** 12 minutes. Press **START** to preheat.

4 When display indicates **ADD FOOD**, place one tray of danishes in middle position. When display says **TURN FOOD**, remove tray and rotate it front to back, but do not turn pies over. **BAKE** until browned and puffy. Transfer to a cooling rack and cool completely. Store leftover danishes in an airtight container. Danishes will stay fresh for up to 3 days.

TIP Chocolate hazelnut spread not your favorite? Try substituting 1 tbsp (15 mL) cream cheese and top with 1 tsp (5 mL) raspberry or sour cherry jam for a fruit and cheese combination.

LYNNE'S CHOCOLATE MOLTEN LAVA CAKES

MAKES 4 SERVINGS

My coworker Lynne went off to the north of France for a week of cooking school and came back with this recipe for amazing lava cakes. I decided we needed to have them in this cookbook, since they make four perfect desserts. The beauty of these lava cakes is that they have a nice and gooey molten middle that is full of yummy chocolate flavor.

PREP TIME
15 minutes

CHILLING TIME
30 minutes or longer

COOK TIME
8 minutes

VORTEX PROGRAM
▶ Bake

Butter for greasing ramekins

4 oz (125 g) dark bittersweet chocolate, chopped

½ cup (125 mL) unsalted butter

½ cup (125 mL) granulated sugar

2 eggs

⅓ cup (75 mL) all-purpose flour

Vanilla ice cream or whipped cream

▶ FOUR ¾-CUP (175 ML) RAMEKINS, BUTTERED

1 Grease four ramekins with butter, including bottom and sides; set aside.

2 In a medium-size bowl, combine chocolate and unsalted butter. Place over a pot of hot water to create a bain-marie, or double boiler, and stir until chocolate and butter are melted. Or melt in a microwave-safe bowl for about 1 minute, stirring every 30 seconds until melted.

3 In a separate bowl, whisk the eggs together with the sugar until thick, then stir in the flour and mix well. Pour the melted chocolate slowly into the egg mixture and mix well.

4 Divide the batter into ramekins and place them on Vortex cooking tray in refrigerator to chill for at least 30 minutes. Using display panel, select **BAKE**, set **TEMPERATURE** to 350°F (180°C) and **TIME** to 13 (for a gooey center) to 14 minutes (for a firmer center). When display indicates **ADD FOOD**, slide cooking tray into middle position. **BAKE** until tops have formed a crust.

5 Remove tray and allow ramekins to rest for 5 minutes. Use a small knife to loosen the cakes from the ramekin and turn them over onto a serving plate. Garnish with vanilla ice cream or whipped cream and fresh berries.

TIPS Use a good-quality chocolate for this recipe. I like the Lindt brand and use the entire (100 g) chocolate bar. Look for a good semi-sweet chocolate.

The ramekins are very hot after they come out of the Vortex. A good clean dish towel works best for getting a grip on the ramekin and turning it upside down to remove the lava cake.

These cakes can be made a day ahead and refrigerated.

HOT CHOCOLATE & CHURROS

MAKES 4 TO 6 SERVINGS

My son Jack used to work in a small Mexican cantina, and their churros were legendary. We decided to try them in the Vortex, since instead it's so much cleaner than all that deep-frying. Thick rich hot chocolate with a texture somewhere between a drink and a sauce accompanies this air-fried version dusted with cinnamon sugar. Make sure to serve the churros as hot as you can and dip them deep into the molten chocolate.

PREP TIME
20 minutes

COOK TIME
10 minutes

VORTEX PROGRAM
▸ **Air Fry**

CHURROS

¼ cup (60 mL) granulated sugar

2 tsp (10 mL) ground cinnamon

2 eggs

1 tsp (5 mL) vanilla

1 cup (250 mL) water

1 tsp (5 mL) salt

1 tbsp (15 mL) butter

1 cup (250 mL) all-purpose flour

Buttery cooking spray

2 tbsp (30 mL) melted butter

▸ PASTRY BAG (PIPING BAG) WITH STAR TIP

1 *Churros:* In a small bowl, combine 3 tbsp (45 mL) sugar with cinnamon; mix well and set aside.

2 In another bowl, beat eggs with vanilla; set aside.

3 In a pot, combine water, salt, remaining 1 tbsp (15 mL) sugar and butter. Bring to a boil, remove from heat and stir in flour all at one time with a wooden spoon. Stir vigorously until the dough is very smooth and pulls away from the sides of the pan, about 2 minutes (it will be very thick). Let cool for 5 minutes, then vigorously mix in the egg vanilla mixture in three portions, beating vigorously each time until completely incorporated into the batter.

4 Lightly spray cooking trays with cooking spray. Spoon the dough into a pastry (piping) bag fitted with a large star tip. Pipe about five 4-inch (10 cm) strips of dough (using a small knife to cut the strips free of the piping tip) onto two cooking trays, leaving enough space around the strips to ensure they are not touching. Spray strips with cooking spray.

5 Using display panel, select **AIR FRY**, set **TEMPERATURE** to 375°F (190°C) and set **TIME** to 10 minutes. When display indicates **ADD FOOD**, slide one cooking tray into middle position. Cook undisturbed for 10 minutes until puffed, brown and set. Repeat with remaining churros.

6 Brush finished warm churros with melted butter. Roll into cinnamon sugar and serve with small bowls of Hot Chocolate.

continued →

HOT CHOCOLATE

6 tbsp (90 mL) cocoa powder

$\frac{1}{8}$ tsp (0.5 mL) cayenne pepper (optional)

3 tbsp (45 mL) granulated sugar

1 tsp (5 mL) cornstarch

1$\frac{1}{2}$ cups (375 mL) whole milk

7 *Hot Chocolate:* In a heavy saucepan, whisk together cocoa, sugar, cornstarch and cayenne, if using. Place the saucepan over low heat and vigorously stir in $\frac{1}{2}$ cup (125 mL) of the milk. When the mixture is smooth, add remaining milk. Bring to a boil over medium-high heat, stirring constantly. Reduce heat to low and simmer for 10 minutes until thickened. Set aside and cover to keep warm.

TIPS When using a pastry (piping) bag, press the mixture down to the bottom of the bag and twist the top of the bag to keep it closed. If you are not used to piping with a pastry bag, a bag clip comes in handy to help keep the bag closed.

When holding a pastry bag, you should squeeze only with your hand that is placed at the top of the bag. The hand that holds the tip is only for guiding the direction of where you want the bag to go.

If chocolate is not your favorite, serve with dulce de leche sauce instead.

"MAKE SURE TO SERVE THE CHURROS AS HOT AS YOU CAN AND DIP THEM DEEP INTO THE MOLTEN CHOCOLATE."

JELLY BOMB DOUGHNUTS

MAKES 6 TO 8 DOUGHNUTS

Doughnuts have taken over the dessert treat market like wildfire. Most doughnuts have to be deep-fried, but this is where the Vortex shines. With just a light spritz of cooking spray, you have a delicious cake-style sweet. My son Jack loves to fill them with seedless raspberry jam, but if custard or glaze is more your style, then go to town.

PREP TIME
2 hours

COOK TIME
7 minutes

VORTEX PROGRAMS
▶ Proof
▶ Air Fry

2 cups (500 mL) all-purpose flour

¼ cup (60 mL) softened butter

1 package (8 g) or 2¼ tsp (11 mL) quick-rising (instant) yeast

3 tbsp (45 mL) granulated sugar

½ tsp (2 mL) salt

½ cup (125 mL) milk, gently warmed (see Tip)

1 large egg

Olive or coconut oil cooking spray

1 cup (250 mL) seedless raspberry jam

▶ PARCHMENT PAPER
▶ ROLLING PIN
▶ PASTRY (PIPING) BAG OR SMALL SEALABLE BAG

1 In a large bowl, combine flour and softened butter. Using your fingers, rub the butter through the flour until it is completely broken up and looks like a shaggy dough. Stir in yeast, sugar and salt; mix well.

2 In a 2-cup (500 mL) measure, whisk together warmed milk and egg. Add to flour mixture and stir with a wooden spoon until mixture can no longer be stirred. Turn out onto a floured surface and knead until the dough is smooth and elastic and only slightly tacky, about 5 minutes. Form into a ball and place in a lightly oiled bowl.

3 Place dough onto drip tray and cover with plastic wrap. Slid into bottom position of cooking chamber. On the display panel, select **PROOF**, set **TEMPERATURE** to 90°F (32°C) and set **TIME** to 60 minutes, or cover and let sit in a warm area at least 1 hour or until dough has doubled in size. If using Vortex without **PROOF** function, follow directions above, cover with clean tea towel and let rise in a warm location about 40 to 60 minutes.

4 Line a baking sheet with parchment paper and lightly spray with oil spray. Turn out dough onto lightly floured work surface and roll out to a ½-inch (1 cm) thick 6- by 8-inch (15 by 20 cm) rectangle.

5 Using a 3-inch (7.5 cm) round doughnut cutter or rim of a glass, cut six to eight doughnuts, kneading scraps together and rerolling into more doughnut rounds. Spray dough rounds on both sides with oil spray and then roll in sugar to coat on both sides. Place doughnuts onto two cooking trays, ensuring they have space around each doughnut, and place in cooking chamber. Select **PROOF**, set **TEMPERATURE** to 90°F (32°C) and set **TIME** to 40 minutes for the second proof. Remove trays from cooking chamber when **PROOF** function is complete. (If your Vortex does not have a **PROOF** function, let rise in a warm location.)

6 Place drip tray in the bottom of cooking chamber. Using the display panel, select **AIR FRY**, adjust **TEMPERATURE** to 375°F (190°C) and set **TIME** to 8 minutes. **PREHEAT** Vortex until display indicates **ADD FOOD**.

7 Slide one cooking tray into middle position and cook until display indicates **TURN FOOD**. Turn doughnuts over and return tray to middle position. Cook until golden. Let cool 5 minutes, then transfer to a wire rack and cool completely. Repeat with second tray.

8 Put jam into a pastry (piping) bag or small sealable bag with the corner snipped off. Using a sharp pointed knife, poke a hole into the side of the doughnut then squeeze in some jam. Serve warm.

TIPS Milk should be warmed only to about 100 to 110°F (38 to 43°C). If you get it too hot, it will kill the yeast and your doughnuts will not rise.

Doughnuts can also be filled with pastry cream, vanilla or chocolate custard, or lemon or lime curd.

MAPLE ROASTED PEARS
WITH BLUE CHEESE

MAKES 2 TO 4 SERVINGS

I love fresh pears partnered with blue cheese on a charcuterie board. So when I had pears and an extra piece of delicious blue cheese in my fridge, I decided to try "roasting" them in the Vortex. The results were delicious, especially when I brushed them before cooking with maple syrup and then added a drizzle afterward too.

PREP TIME
5 minutes

COOK TIME
10 minutes

VORTEX PROGRAMS
▶ Air Fry

2 ripe pears

1 tbsp (15 mL) butter, melted

1 tsp (5 mL) maple syrup

Crumbled blue cheese

Maple syrup for drizzling

1 Cut pears in half lengthwise, then use a measuring spoon or melon baller to remove the core. Remove stem. Brush pears with butter and maple syrup and place on cooking tray cut side up.

2 Place drip tray in bottom of cooking chamber. Using display panel, select **AIR FRY**, adjust **TEMPERATURE** to 400°F (200°C) and set **TIME** to 10 minutes.

3 Cook undisturbed until pears have softened and are hot. Remove from cooking chamber and serve with a crumbled blue cheese, if using, and an additional drizzle of maple syrup.

TIPS If blue cheese is not your favorite, serve with a dollop of vanilla Greek yogurt or ice cream, or just on their own.

SALTED CARAMEL ROCKY ROAD CHOCOLATE CAKE

MAKES ONE 8-INCH (20 CM) CAKE

For such a long name, this has to be the easiest cake to make, because you prepare and bake it all in one pan. It's so moist and delicious, and the topping takes it over the top. One serving gives you a big burst of chocolate flavor.

PREP TIME

15 minutes

COOK TIME

30 minutes

VORTEX PROGRAM

▶ Bake

▶ Broil

⅓ cup (75 mL) vegetable oil

2 oz (60 g) unsweetened baking chocolate

1⅓ cups (325 mL) all-purpose flour

⅔ cup (150 mL) granulated sugar

¾ cup (175 mL) water

½ tsp (2 mL) baking soda

½ tsp (2 mL) salt

1 egg, lightly beaten

1 cup (250 mL) salted caramel chips

2 cups (500 mL) mini marshmallows

¼ cup (60 mL) chopped pecans (optional)

▶ 8- BY 8-INCH (20 BY 20 CM) BAKING PAN

1 Place oil and chocolate in 8- by 8-inch (20 by 20 cm) baking pan. Turn one of the cooking trays upside down in the bottom position of the cooking chamber. Using the display panel, select BAKE, adjust TEMPERATURE to 325°F (160°C) and set TIME to 2 minutes.

2 When display indicates ADD FOOD, place baking pan in the cooking chamber and CLOSE DOOR. When timer goes off, remove pan.

3 Add flour, sugar, water, baking soda, salt and egg to oil and chocolate mixture; using a fork or whisk, stir until well blended.

4 Reset display panel TIME to 25 minutes (cooking function and temperature remains the same) and press START. When displays indicates ADD FOOD, place cake pan back on cooking tray. When timer goes off, remove cake from cooking chamber and sprinkle with salted caramel chips, marshmallows and nuts, if using.

5 Using display panel, select BROIL. Allow Vortex to preheat, then when display says ADD FOOD, place cake back in cooking chamber. Set TIME for 2 minutes and broil just until marshmallows are golden and toothpick inserted in center of cake comes out clean.

TIPS This cake can also be made in an 8-inch (20 cm) round pan.

If salted caramel is not your favorite, try substituting dark or milk chocolate, butterscotch, white chocolate or peanut butter chips instead.

Unsweetened chocolate is a solid baking chocolate made from cocoa solids and cocoa butter. It is not a popular choice for eating since it has a very bitter taste, but it's a perfect choice for this cake because it adds a strong chocolate flavor.

SIMPLE APPLE CRISP

MAKES 6 SERVINGS

A true classic favorite, this easy apple crisp is a reminder of generations past. It all comes together quickly, so pop it into the Vortex and wait for the delicious smell to waft through the house. I love it with a scoop of vanilla ice cream and a drizzle of salted caramel sauce.

PREP TIME
20 minutes

COOK TIME
20 minutes

VORTEX PROGRAM
▶ Bake

APPLES

6 cups (1.5 L) peeled, sliced or chopped apples, such as Golden Delicious, Granny Smith or Courtland

1/3 cup (75 mL) granulated sugar

1 1/2 tsp (7 mL) ground cinnamon

1/4 tsp (1 mL) ground nutmeg

TOPPING

1 cup (250 mL) rolled oats

1/3 cup (75 mL) packed brown sugar

1/2 tsp (2 mL) ground cinnamon

1/3 cup (75 mL) cold butter, cut into small cubes

Vanilla ice cream or whipping cream

▶ 8-INCH (20 CM) SQUARE OR ROUND BAKING DISH
▶ PASTRY BLENDER

1 *Apples:* Place apples in bottom of baking dish. Sprinkle with sugar, cinnamon and nutmeg; toss to coat.

2 *Topping:* In a bowl, combine oats, brown sugar and cinnamon. Add butter and, using a pastry blender, cut the butter into the oat mixture until mixture resembles pea-sized crumbs. (Alternatively, you can use your hands to cut butter into the mixture.)

3 Spread topping over apples in baking dish and gently pat to even it out.

4 Slide a cooking tray into the bottom position, upside down, so baking pan has a flat surface to sit on. Using the display panel, select BAKE, adjust TEMPERATURE to 350°F (180°C) and set TIME to 20 minutes. Press START to preheat.

5 When Vortex displays ADD FOOD, place baking pan on top of cooking tray. BAKE until topping is golden brown and apples are bubbly.

6 Serve warm with vanilla ice cream.

TIP You can add 1/2 cup (125 mL) chopped nuts such as walnuts, pecans or almonds to the topping if you like.

SWEET CHERRY HAND PIES

MAKES 6 SERVINGS

I have to admit, when I was a kid, I was a fan of the cherry hand pie you could get from the hamburger chain with the golden arches! In fact, I am a total cherry fanatic; someone actually suggested to my mother that's what I should be called when I was born — Cherry Pye. So while testing this recipe, I indulged in my secret obsession and ate all of them myself!

PREP TIME
15 minutes

COOK TIME
15 minutes

VORTEX PROGRAM
▶ Bake

---

1 lb (500 g) whole fresh or frozen pitted sweet cherries (thawed if frozen)

1/3 cup (75 mL) granulated sugar

1 tbsp (15 mL) cornstarch

Zest and juice of 1 lemon

1 egg yolk

1 tbsp (15 mL) water

1 package (1 lb/500 g) frozen butter puff pastry sheets, thawed in refrigerator

Turbinado sugar for decorating (optional)

1 Place a colander over a bowl and add cherries. Sprinkle over sugar, cornstarch, lemon zest and juice; stir to combine. Allow cherries to sit for 15 minutes over colander to allow some of the excess juice to run off and ensure your filling isn't too liquidy. Reserve drained cherry juice and place in a small saucepan.

2 Over medium-high heat, bring cherry juice to a boil. Whisk constantly for 2 minutes until thickened. Remove from heat and allow mixture to cool.

3 In a bowl, beat together egg yolk and water; mix well and set aside.

4 Unroll one sheet of puff pastry and cut into six rectangles, about 3 by 4 inches (7.5 by 10 cm). Place rectangles on cooking trays, using two trays and working quickly to keep puff pastry as cool as possible. Cut the second sheet into the same size rectangles and place them in the refrigerator to keep cold; these will be the tops of the pies.

5 Spoon about 2 tbsp (30 mL) cherry filling onto the bottom rectangles, and drizzle with a little of the thickened cherry juice. Brush bottom edges with egg wash, then top with the chilled rectangles from the second sheet of puff pastry. Using a fork, crimp the edges of the pastry to seal them. Cut two or three slashes into the top of pies with a serrated knife.

6 Brush egg wash over each hand pie. Sprinkle with turbinado sugar, if using. Place pies in the freezer for 15 minutes to chill.

7 Using display panel, select **BAKE**, adjust **TEMPERATURE** to 360°F (182°C) and set **TIME** to 11 minutes. Press **START** to preheat.

8 When Vortex indicates **ADD FOOD**, place one tray of pies in middle position. When indicator says **TURN FOOD**, remove tray and rotate it back to front, but do not turn pies over. **BAKE** until browned and puffy. Transfer to a cooling rack and cool completely. Store leftover hand pies in an airtight container. Pies will stay fresh for up to 3 days.

TIPS You can make ahead the hand pies, then freeze before baking. Cook straight from frozen, adding 5 minutes to total cooking time.

I used frozen, pitted cherries to develop this recipe, but when they are in season, be sure to use fresh. You will need to pit the cherries first, though. Be sure to leave them whole; otherwise they will leak too much juice.

WHITE CHOCOLATE BLONDIES

MAKES ONE 8- BY 8-INCH (20 BY 20 CM) PAN

Buttery, soft, chewy and loaded with white chocolate chips, these cookie bars are loaded with flavor and the perfect snack when you need dessert in a pinch. Blondies are occasionally referred to as blonde brownies because they are made without cocoa powder or chocolate, and aspire to a rich vanilla flavor.

PREP TIME
15 minutes

COOK TIME
30 minutes

VORTEX PROGRAM
▶ Bake

½ cup (125 mL) unsalted butter, melted

1 cup (250 mL) packed brown sugar

2 tsp (10 mL) vanilla

1 egg, lightly beaten

1 cup (250 mL) all-purpose flour

½ tsp (2 mL) baking powder

¼ tsp (1 mL) salt

⅛ tsp (0.5 mL) baking soda

½ cup (125 mL) white chocolate chips

▶ 8- BY 8-INCH SQUARE (20 BY 20 CM) BAKING PAN

1 Lightly grease and flour an 8- by 8-inch (20 by 20 cm) baking pan; set aside.

2 In a bowl, combine melted butter and brown sugar; whisk together until smooth. Add in vanilla and egg and blend until smooth.

3 In a separate bowl, combine flour, baking powder, salt and baking soda; stir into butter mixture, then add white chocolate chips. Mix until a smooth batter is formed and pour into prepared pan.

4 Slide drip pan into bottom position upside down so that the baking pan has a flat surface to sit on. Using display panel, select **BAKE**, adjust **TEMPERATURE** to 325°F (160°C) and set **TIME** to 30 minutes. Select **START**. When display indicates **ADD FOOD**, place baking pan on drip pan in cooking chamber. Close door and bake until tester inserted in the center comes out clean.

5 Transfer to a cooling rack and allow blondies to cool before cutting.

TIPS Where brownies depend on chocolate for their flavor, for blondies it's all about the brown sugar. This is what gives them their distinctive molasses flavor. I suggest using dark brown sugar, but light is fine too.

Not a fan of white chocolate? Consider replacing the white chocolate chips with chopped nuts, such as walnuts or pecans, or other flavored baking chips, like butterscotch, peanut butter or salted caramel.

Once cooled, blondies can be stored in an airtight container at room temperature. They will keep for about 1 week. To freeze, wrap the sliced blondies in freezer-safe wrap and transfer to an airtight container or sealable freezer bag. Store for up to 3 months. Thaw first before eating.

Library and Archives Canada Cataloguing in Publication

Title: Essential Instant Vortex Air Fryer Oven cookbook : 100 recipes for air frying, roasting, dehydrating, rotisserie & more / Donna-Marie Pye.
Other titles: 100 recipes for air frying, roasting, dehydrating, rotisserie & more | One hundred recipes for air frying, roasting, dehydrating, rotisserie & more
Names: Pye, Donna-Marie, author.
Description: "Official Instant book."
Identifiers: Canadiana 20200277766 | ISBN 9780778806745 (softcover)
Subjects: LCSH: Hot air frying. | LCSH: Cooking. | LCGFT: Cookbooks.
Classification: LCC TX689 .P94 2020 | DDC 641.7/7—dc23

INDEX